Praise for *Roots, Branches & Spirits*

"Be prepared to be transported as Byron Ballard expertly weaves stories and practice, blending tradition and modern magical innovation all at once."   —Laura Tempest Zakroff, author of *Weave the Liminal*

"Leave your preconceived notions about Appalachia and its people at the door and let Byron Ballard take you on a journey from Scotland to Ulster to the mountains of the southern United States. *Roots, Branches & Spirits* presents a magic born of necessity and skillfully adapted to the place where it was—and still is—practiced."
—John Beckett, author of *The Path of Paganism*

"Part history, part folklore, and part spellwork and ritual, Byron Ballard shares with us the rich customs of her forebears, from women's kitchen magic to burial practices to the use of herbs and stones."
—Patti Wigington, author of *Herb Magic* and *Badass Ancestors*

"H. Byron Ballard takes us on another engaging journey into the mountainous rural United States, where the worlds of magic, phantoms, and old traditions continue to flourish well into the twenty-first century."
—Christopher Orapello, coauthor of *Besom, Stang & Sword*, artist, and cohost of the *Down at the Crossroads* podcast

"A delightful breath of fresh mountain air in which H. Byron Ballard invites us to explore a magical practice that's ingrained in the land, flourishes in the rivers and creeks, and whispers secrets on the breeze. A world where sprite and spirit, fact and legend, merge seamlessly with herb and remedy and receipt to create a magic all its own."
—Dorothy Morrison, author of *Everyday Magic* and *Utterly Wicked*

"A lovingly constructed quilt of culture and magic, land and spirit, written by a woman whose roots go as deep as an oak's into the mountains where she was born and raised, while her branches dance in the sun and wind of our shared humanity."
—Diotima M̶ ̶ ̶ ̶ ̶iss the Sky

"A wonderfully detailed walk down the winding mountain paths of witchery found in [Ballard's] Appalachia. From word one, she takes you firmly by the hand and guides you through the rich history of the region—unveiling her collected folklore, ancestral remedies, and practical workings as she goes along, exploring rabbit trails at every crossing and turn."

—Tara-Love Maguire, coauthor of *Besom, Stang, and Sword*

"*Roots, Branches & Spirits* bursts forth with magic on every page. H. Byron Ballard gives us an in-depth look at the enchanted world of Appalachia as only she can. ... I highly recommend *Roots, Branches & Spirits* as a welcome addition to any library."

—Lilith Dorsey, author *Orishas, Goddesses and Voodoo Queens*

"This is not a book—it's a portal to a place. ... The pages open up and transport the reader to the forests, the river, the haunted places, or granny's kitchen table, where you feel welcome, and maybe learn a remedy or two."

—Angie Buchanan, cofounder and senior minister of Earth Traditions and founder of the Death Midwife

"Byron Ballard effortlessly blends her knowledge of the history of her home region, her insightful analysis of the impacts of the past, and her practical witchcraft. Reading this book feels like sitting at a big table having a conversation with this expert of both folkways and witchery."

—Cyndi Brannen, author of *Keeping Her Keys*

"Byron Ballard's deep Appalachian roots, and her genuine love for her homeland, its people, and their ways, is a bright beacon that illuminates the path through this book."

—Sara Mastros, author of *Orphic Hymns Grimoire*

"Filled with personal musings, historical details, and magical suggestions for both the novice and the knowledgeable, this is a book for those who love their land-base and those who are new to the practice of that ancient art."

—Hecate Demetersdatter, www.hecatedemeter.wordpress.com

Roots
Branches
& Spirits

About the Author

H. Byron Ballard, BA, MFA, is a western North Carolina native, teacher, folklorist, and writer. She has served as a featured speaker and teacher at Sacred Space Conference, Pagan Spirit Gathering, Southeast Wise Women's Herbal Conference, Glastonbury Goddess Conference, Heartland, Sirius Rising, Starwood, Scottish Pagan Federation Conference, HexFest, and other gatherings. She is senior priestess and cofounder of Mother Grove Goddess Temple and the Coalition of Earth Religions for Education and Support (CERES), both in Asheville, NC.

Her essays are featured in several anthologies, and she writes a regular column for *SageWoman* magazine. Byron is currently at work on *The Ragged Wound: Tending the Soul of Appalachia* (a book examining the current state of the Appalachian region) for Smith Bridge Press, a novel called *Wild Magic, Wide Wonder*, and a book on permaculture for Pagans. Visit her website at www.myvillagewitch.com.

Roots Branches & Spirits

The Folkways & Witchery of Appalachia

H. Byron Ballard

FOREWORD BY
Alex Bledsoe

Llewellyn Publications
Woodbury, Minnesota

FIRST EDITION
Fourth Printing, 2023

Cover design by Shannon McKuhen
Cover illustration by Jerry Hoare / Donna Rosen Artist Representative
Interior art element by the Llewellyn Art Department

Llewellyn Publications is a registered trademark of Llewellyn Worldwide Ltd.

Library of Congress Cataloging-in-Publication Data
Names: Ballard, H. Byron, author.
Title: Roots, branches & spirits : the folkways & witchery of Appalachia / H. Byron Ballard.
Description: First edition. | Woodbury, Minnesota : Llewellyn Publications, 2021. | Includes bibliographical references. | Summary: "A survey of the spiritual customs and traditions of the people of the southern highlands of Appalachia"—provided by publisher.
Identifiers: LCCN 2020047222 (print) | LCCN 2020047223 (ebook) | ISBN 9780738764535 | ISBN 9780738764849 (ebook)
Subjects: LCSH: Appalachian Region—Religious life and customs. | Appalachian Region—Folklore.
Classification: LCC BR535 .B35 2021 (print) | LCC BR535 (ebook) | DDC 248.0975—dc23
LC record available at https://lccn.loc.gov/2020047222
LC ebook record available at https://lccn.loc.gov/2020047223

Llewellyn Publications
A Division of Llewellyn Worldwide Ltd.
2143 Wooddale Drive
Woodbury, MN 55125-2989
www.llewellyn.com

Printed in the United States of America

Also by H. Byron Ballard

Staubs and Ditchwater
(Smith Bridge Press, 2012)

Asfidity and Mad-Stones
(Smith Bridge Press, 2015)

*Embracing Willendorf: A Witch's Way of
Loving Your Body to Health & Fitness*
(Smith Bridge Press, 2017)

Earth Works: Ceremonies in Tower Time
(Smith Bridge Press, 2018)

Dedication

This book is dedicated to one of my ancestors, a woman who looms large in my family mythology. She was small of stature and stout, and I've never seen a photo of her as a young woman, before all the children. In my mind's eye, she still wanders the steep streets of old West End with a dented dishpan, picking dandelion greens and young pokeweed. She died there too, before I was born and before I came to live uphill from her house at Number Ten Roberts Street. This book is dedicated to Lillian, Grandma Westmoreland.

Acknowledgments

My gratitude goes out to a slew of people who kept me upright and moving forward as I dove deep into this Pandora's box of history and practice: my homefolks, Kat and Joe; my mountain magic bringers, Crystal, Kate D., Michelle H., Marilyn McMinn-McCredie, and Renee'; my Wisteria family; Cassandra Latham-Jones and Laetitia Latham-Jones; my work-wives at Asheville Raven and Crone; Brian, my work-husband on the road; the Wyrd Mountain Gals team of Alicia Corbin Knighten, Gomez the Yardman, and Craig Steven of SunSlice Records; and the Llewellyn team, Heather Greene, Shannon McKuhen, Donna Burch-Brown, Lauryn Heineman, Andy Belmas, and Jake-Ryan Kent. Special thanks to Gerald Milnes, whose early book on Appalachian witchery, *Signs, Cures, and Witchery: German Appalachian Folklore*, is still a handy reference. To all the Appalachian women who plied their trade in these old hills—who caught the babies and cured warts and blew the fire out of a burn, who sang their grandmother's laments and told and retold the old stories—I am not worthy of your powerful legacy. But I will do my best to honor all that you have passed down to me.

Disclaimer on the Use of Herbs, Oils, and Such

The herbs, oils, remedies, and the like contained within these pages are offered as a representation of traditional folklore and are not intended to diagnose, treat, or cure any conditions or diseases.

A Note on Bible Quotes Used in This Book

All verses contained here are from the King James version of the Bible. It is the traditional choice in much of southern Appalachia and is the one I grew up with, and I prefer it because the language is evocative and beautiful.

Contents

Foreword

My father's family hails from the mountains of East Tennessee. There's even a Bledsoe County just north of Chattanooga, and if you turn over a rock in Jonesborough (home of the National Storytelling Festival, as mentioned in chapter 3), you're as likely to find a Bledsoe as a copperhead. Depending on the situation, they both might bite you. I've written six novels set in these mountains, and as part of that I've studied many of the same things Byron covers in this book. So when I tell you that this book is the real deal, I know whereof I speak: like Byron, I'm from so far south that, for us, *sushi* means "bait." I've known Byron Ballard for a while now and have crossed paths with her at various events across the South. Her warmth and kindness are legendary, and I've experienced them firsthand. But more than that, her dedication to her home region and its people is the kind of all-encompassing championing that we need. Her determination to uncover and document the practices and beliefs of this region, *her* region, are, in the fullest sense of the word, invaluable.

Why do I say that? Because this is the way people survived before technology and encroaching modernity made such things, at least temporarily, unnecessary. But as we're starting to finally learn, this artificiality that was created to enhance our quality of life may do more harm than good. We're damn near enslaved to our devices, to food that magically appears on demand, to constant mental and emotional stimulation, to a belief that what we *want* is what we *need*. When and if all this modernity collapses, the skills, practices, and beliefs Byron describes here might be more important than we realize.

And even if that doesn't happen, knowing how to flake your mica without going blind surely can't hurt.

A hundred or so years ago, the folks who traveled into the mountains to find and record its music were known as "songcatchers." In these pages, Byron refers to herself as a "spellcatcher," acquiring and preserving the habits, rituals, and details that make this way of life so special. As I write this, I'm sitting at home practicing social distancing, and the self-sufficient ways of Byron's book seem even more necessary and crucial.

What Byron has done here, and with her work in general, is collect, collate, and present information that might otherwise have been lost. You who are reading this book, you lucky dog, will benefit from her wisdom, insight, humor, and determination. And your job of work, if you choose to accept it, will be to pass on what you've learned to the next generation of seekers. In one of my favorite movies, Walter Hill's *Crossroads*, bluesman Joe Seneca tells Ralph Macchio, "You got to take the music *past* where you found it." That's also the implied duty of those who embrace these roots, branches, and spirits.

Alex Bledsoe
April 2020

Introduction

The germination of this idea—to honor the skills and stories of the people who came before us in Appalachia—appeared years ago when I recognized my intractable connection to this region. When I am not writing about the rich and troubled culture that birthed and sustains me, I am traveling, teaching, listening, and gathering tales and folkways.

It truly began in my childhood when I spent summer days in a cove with hairy ponies and winter days in a cold and drafty house without a bathroom. That cove upbringing gave me much of the stonework that forms my foundation—sweet water, gravel roads, big trees, and bigger secrets. So many secrets. When people lament how peculiar the world has become and long for a return to a more wholesome time, I spit out a bitter little laugh. The dominant culture has never been easy on people like me and mine. We have learned down the long generations that we must find our desired sweetness and our ease in whatever way we can—in the tune of a half-remembered ballad, in the abundance of late fall apples, and in the arms and thighs of the land itself.

The southern highlands are near the bottom of the old Appalachian chain. We sit on the solid lap of some of the oldest mountains in the world, and the effect is profound on those of us who are attached to the twisty roots that bind us to this land, to these places. The word *wisdom* has become a hard one to piece into the jigsaw puzzle of the language. The more I read it and hear it, the less meaning it seems to have for me. It gets used for everything from cars to yoga gear. But these hills have something ineffable and abiding that sits beneath the level of stone and clay and permeates the water of spring and creek and river.

The biological diversity of the Appalachian bioregion is well-documented. That diversity extends to the people as well as their collective folkways. In this book, I concentrate on the folkways I know and practice. When something is outside my personal experience, I will note that. These revenants may vary depending on the family and the area of occupation. These are the traditional ways I learned and have come to respect and love.

In addition, the Appalachian region is large, encompassing twelve states in the United States and part of Canada. My scope is the southern highlands, which is the section that includes western North Carolina, eastern Tennessee, southwest Virginia, northern Georgia and Alabama, and parts of Kentucky, Ohio, and West Virginia. Some things—like the devastation of various extraction practices—are common to most of the region. Others are more limited geographically but no less important culturally. Although parts of Appalachia are in the South, it is not necessarily "Southern," which implies a homogeneity that also isn't true for the South as a whole. The regional "feel" is different, the dialects and accents are different, and, of course, the culture is different.

The spiritual practices of Appalachia, or at least this part of it, are rooted in a strongly held and direct Protestant Christianity.

When I was growing up in west (by god!) Buncombe County, there was little reason to ask acquaintances their religion. They were either Baptist or Methodist with a smattering of other Protestant sects thrown in, or they were unchurched, as I was. *Unchurched* is code for a family falling out with a pastor or congregation and never finding another church home to replace the one lost. It gave my family an odd sort of foundation in cultural Christianity without the burden of either dogma or practice. But I have seen serpents handled in a church that was in the high country, somewhere in that crotch of land that holds a little of Tennessee, a bit of Virginia, and some shreds of North Carolina. That was a moment of intense divine connection that I will never likely forget.

There is much to relish in the preserved folkways of these people, who are hardworking when there are jobs to work. But we bear an almost imperceptible twilight about us. Whether this is the result of our genetic makeup or our history is hard to tell. The result is a strange fatalism and resignation. You can hear it in the music, in regional writing, in the stories of haints and boogers that stalk our region. The handwrought quilts that are made from leftover bits of flour sacking and this year's new shirt tell another story of women's work made art, of utilitarian objects made beautiful and harmonious, almost by accident.

This writing then comes from the darkest and truest part of me—a part that is never healed and never entirely broken. If you choose to make your way along with me, you will find the voyage ragged, and the wayfaring signs may not be entirely clear. But in the end you will know something of this land, its history, and the folks that dwell here, whether in body or spirit.

We will look at the hauntings and the revenants, from folk healing to the common magic that flows from the holiest of ghosts. You will come away with old-fashioned, stained, and torn recipe cards that may give you a taste of this place, its people, and the magic we use to survive when thriving is not an option granted to the likes of us.

Many Americans trace their ancestry back to this region, so many that I refer to them as the Appalachian diaspora. Some left because of family dynamics; more left because there wasn't any work available. They migrated north to the Rust Belt and west into the oil fields of Texas and Oklahoma. The ones I've met in my travels long wistfully for a time and a place that were never literally theirs.

Come with me now to this place that smells of rot and tobacco spit, mountain mint and kerosene. If you are from this place, welcome. If you are away from this place that holds the bones and stories of your ancestors, welcome home. And if you are here simply due to unrepentant curiosity, a need, or a sense of adventure, you are also very welcome indeed.

Part 1
Beginnings

Chapter 1

Old Mountains, New Worlds

I think of myself as a forensic folklorist—a person who reads between the lines of legends to discover the truth of the myth within. A couple of years ago I was fortunate to work in the Alexander Carmichael collection at the University of Edinburgh as I continued my journey into the various roots of the Appalachian folk magic that is both my practice and my study. My heart is in the hollows and on the ridges of my native land—I stand on the stooped shoulders of all the yarb women and cove doctors who came before me, and I stand in solidarity with the folks who are preserving these practices in this present and challenging time.

We will explore one of the most beautiful, misunderstood, and abused regions of North America—our region, Appalachia. Myth and history, heart and hands. For this region is old and new, a renewed weaving of an old coverlet. Perhaps I can tempt you into the sheer joy that is this vibrant and misunderstood culture and engage you in a renewal of its old folkways in this new and troubled world.

I come from a land both rich and poor, beloved and despised. To be an Appalachian native is to be "othered" almost everywhere you go. There will be many opportunities to explain the stereotypes, to talk about The Beverly Hillbillies and corrupt politicians and coal mining. People like me are used to code-switching—to suppressing our accents when we feel we have to, to "pass" for something we aren't. To be from Appalachia—and have (as some think) the bad luck to have remained here—is something beyond the understanding of many Americans outside the region. It's acceptable to vacation here, to own a second or third home here. But to claim a deeply rooted ancestry in Appalachia is to invite scorn, mistrust, and mockery, encompassed in the phrase "Paddle faster, I hear banjos."

On the southern horizon, ever present in my life here, rises Mt. Pisgah and the Rat. I grew up on stories of that distinctively shaped mountain and spent much of my teen years driving the curving road of Pisgah Highway, too fast, too confident. Pisgah and the Rat is part of the warp and weft of our folklore, but to dig past the story fed to tourists and other outlanders is to expose the rocky layers of Christianity and colonization that permeate the region. To understand Mt. Pisgah in western North Carolina is to bear witness to genocide and indifference, to hold a vessel that is ancient and modern. This is a microcosm of all of Appalachia but especially here where there is no coal, only jewels. Still the people are lost and hopeless, with rubies in the ground at their feet.

To understand Mt. Pisgah is to visit Deuteronomy, specifically chapter 3. I don't follow biblical teaching, being neither Jewish (those for whom these books of Moses were supposedly written) nor Christian. Peculiar to have been raised here and not be an adherent to one or the other popular flavors of Protestant Christianity, but there it is. I was born into a lapsed Methodist family on my mother's side and a lapsed Baptist one on my father's side. That unbaptized and unchurched status has afforded me many freedoms, most of which I've tasted, many to excess.

The children of Israel, as you may recall from Sunday school or vacation Bible school class (or from that awful Charlton Heston movie we always watched at Easter), wandered about in the desert for forty years following their freedom from bondage in Egypt, bondage not meaning then what it does now. Forty years to travel a few hundred miles, as punishment for golden calf shenanigans and the Twelve Spies lying about the land of milk and honey. Moses had led his people out of bondage in Egypt and across Sinai to the land their god had promised them.

This land was fertile and the landscape held water sources, vineyards, and pastureland. Dreaming of such a place while cursed to wander in the desert must've been a sort of respite along the way. Let's focus on that land as a dream, as a vision of a hopeful future. Let's also not forget that both lands—the mythical one in the Middle East and the one that straddles two counties in western North Carolina—had another thing in common. While undoubtedly fecund, they were also occupied.

After all that bondage-breaking and traveling, Moses was not allowed to enter this rich and promised land. My sources couldn't quite agree on why. Possibly because he broke the original Ten Commandments, but the answer seems to lie in another Old Testament book, Numbers. In the desert of Zin, the god of Abraham specifically told him to speak to this particular rock, the Meribah, and it would give the people water. Instead, he struck it twice with his staff. The rock did produce water and the people quenched their thirsts. But because he disobeyed direct orders, Moses could only view the promised land from the top of Mt. Pisgah. (Some scholars say Mt. Pisgah is the same as Mt. Nebo. There's a Nebo here too—southeast of our Mt. Pisgah.) Moses gazed upon that golden valley and died, probably from disappointment and annoyance.

Fast-forward to the eighteenth century and to this old, soft mountain range, with this hill with its peculiarly lumpy ridge-line. The Reverend George Newton is credited with naming the mountain because the land around it was lush and beautiful, a metaphorical land of milk and honey. This land—these southern highlands—were seen in the same abundant light, hence the renaming of the mountain and ridge. As with many naturally occurring oddities, Pisgah and the Rat lends itself to clinging shreds of folklore, looming large on the horizon and in the imagination.

The Rat creeps up the side of the mountain, like the mouse on the nursery rhyme's clock. Consider that for a moment and imagine living in a world where a mouse running up a clock or a huge rat running up a mountain is a natural but notable occurrence. Any of us who have lived in an old house or a country house or substandard urban housing know the scrambling, scratching sound of a visiting mouse and can easily recognize the predations of its larger cousin the rat. Even as we look to renew our connection—or establish one—with these ancient mountains, we can be squeamish about sharing our living space with other animals, especially those we consider unwholesome or dangerous. Modern humankind, with its intentional quest to be separate from and superior to nature, is the real disease vector. In our sad and impossible quest to separate from land, history, and people, we lose so much that cannot easily be regained.

The Appalachian Mountains and their cultures are the constant butt of jokes throughout the rest of the country. It is one reason I don't use words like *hillbilly* and *backwoods* in mixed company. It often sparks an odd distancing effect that horror film buffs call "urbanoia"—the paranoia of the city-dweller about rural or wild places and the people who live there. This does little to instruct outsiders about the true nature of the culture or to elevate the shame of so many of the region's inhabitants. That self-loathing finds its historical expression in mass migration out of the region, in pained and painful memoirs, and in a lost generation of meth-addicted people.

Appalachia has long been a region of subsistence, creativity, and resilience, however. As the long-toxic extraction industry that is coal mining and its affiliates leaves the region it has despoiled for over a century, a vacuum forms. As the harsh and powerful Protestant religions loosen their grip on the people as those old-time adherents die off, it creates a space, making an opportunity for something new, and frankly healthier, to ride through this land of forest and smoke.

Many people, including those outside the region, are looking to older traditions of herbal healing, farming, and food preservation for clues about proceeding to not only live but figure out how to survive in the Appalachian Mountains' future.

These are some of the oldest mountains in the world, and some of the oldest rivers in the world run through them. According to the Blue Ridge National Heritage organization, the New River and the French Broad River are older than the mountains themselves.[1]

New arrivals and visitors who come for the land (and not merely for the craft beer) are often struck with the feel of the place—hills old and low but somehow filled with a perceived power. Spurious urban myths arise with some frequency and feature a vortex here or a giant crystal buried there, but this is generally nonsense spun by profiteers or folks with agendas of their own. Some of them did feel something, though, and are looking

---

1. "French Broad River," Blue Ridge National Heritage Area, accessed June 23, 2020, https://www.blueridgeheritage.com/destinations/french-broad-river/.

for explanations in the iconic popular culture. The real story is much more complicated—and radically simpler.

The United States is a much-vaunted "melting pot" of cultures and ethnicities. Here at the beginning of the twenty-first century it is also a land of nomads moving from their place of birth to various places of raising to college to jobs in various cities. The idea that several generations of the same family could or would choose to live in close proximity to one another has become an old-fashioned and unworkable notion. Employment, spouses, or toxic familial relationships take the young far from their genesis and into the wide world from whence they will only return for occasional holidays, weddings, and funerals.

This rootlessness is an interesting phenomenon, especially for those of us who were brought up in insular communities where your every move was judged and secrets could be rarely kept. In this strange land where rats climb mountains and unknowable lights skitter along ridgelines and forest floors, there still abide people who claim a long lineage in a central geographic location. This land is a holdover to another time: one of kindred bonds that are almost unbreakable, where blood feuds can transcend generations, and where old women carry secret knowledge. Here your mother's mother might hold the mysteries of birthing, healing, and death. Here midwifery is a set of skills held with humility as well as a strange sort of pride. Here a woman can go out into the weedy edges of church parking lots, a tattoo joint, or a fast food parking lot and gather green plants for a remedy or for supper. These skills are much needed in the shifting chaos of the world, and we will go in search of some of them in these pages as it is made manifest right before our faces, hidden in plain sight.

Over a decade ago I was honored to present a paper at a colloquium at Harvard University. The gathering was called "Forging Folklore: Witches, Pagans, and Neo-Tribal Cultures" and was hosted by the Committee on Degrees in Folklore and Mythology. I presented a paper called "Hillfolks' Hoodoo and the Question of Cultural Strip-Mining." It was a heady weekend and I met a handful of colleagues there who have become lifelong friends. It was a significant turning point in my outlook and my work.

The phrase *cultural strip-mining* was coined by traditional mountain storyteller Marilyn McMinn-McCredie, with whom I worked some years back. Cultural strip-mining is the act of extracting folkways from a culture while returning little or nothing to it. People from outside the culture suck up what they find appealing or can monetize and let the rest fall away or die beneath the wheels of progress. The culture gains little from the exchange and gives up precious materials that leave it weakened in some ineffable way.

When I teach classes in Appalachian folkways—including healing and magic—I am always careful to speak at length about the diversity and richness of the various cultures that make up Appalachia. Cultures. Plural. Many cultures. All those people who think the mountains are full of *Beverly Hillbillies* characters need to think again. I remember the delight I felt when artist and priestess Valeria Watson introduced me to the concept of "Affrilachia." There have been people of African descent here for a very long time. Obviously, the Native Americans were here and the beauty and remoteness of the region have attracted many others. Some were brought here as enslaved or indentured people. Many sought out the mountain fastnesses because they wanted solitude for reasons of their own. Some were running from misdeeds elsewhere. Each group brings a different thread into the weaving that is Appalachia.

The outside world—the citizens of which I grew up calling "outlanders" and "flatlanders"—finds much here to delight in. The views from Parkway to Skyway will take your breath away, especially in autumn. Warming air after rain or a damp night brings wisps of mist that rise to become clouds. Predicted snowstorms may miss us entirely, and storms that were predicted to go north will happily dump a foot of snow, effectively shutting us down for twenty-four hours. Weather can't be scheduled, as we have discovered in this time of shifting climate norms.

There is one thing all mountain people know about this land. Old as it is, the weather upon it is changeable and impactful. In this temperate rain forest, with its crags, hollows, and coves, predicting the weather is challenging as the weather is fickle. Working with the land and the weather patterns that affect it requires attention, experience, and luck, and that is reflected in folkways centering on weather.

This is my Appalachia, and I will take your hand, guide you through, and show you some treasures. But I must warn you that I am a generations-long denizen of this place and there will be stories and songs along the way. For now we will take the poorly maintained trail to the top of Mt. Pisgah.

Not as high as Mt. Mitchell nor as picturesque a walk as the one to Craggy Gardens, this trail has felt the tread of so many feet, human and otherwise. From here we can observe the changes in the landscape for quite a long way. Rippling like waves, the blue ridges go on and on, blocking our road to the horizon but not our view.

Driving into my part of the southern highlands from either east or west, there are places on the highway where the first real view of the mountains happens. That glimpse of that blue ridge makes my heart jerk a little bit, every time. I am of this place and that is often in sharp contrast to those who have come here in more recent times. My work is about these mountains and of these mountains, and these pages will turn on those traditions. The love of this place is wide as well as deep, and new people who understand this land have come to gradually absorb the energy of the region. Some of us are choosing to teach and write about this place in order to mitigate any cultural strip-mining and disrespect that may be a temptation. To look down your nose on a place where so much is willingly shared is to show yourself ill-mannered, greedy, and small.

In the 1960s, a school project in north Georgia turned into an encyclopedic collection of Appalachian history and folk skills that came to be called the Foxfire books. Badly behaved and willful students were sent back to their family elders to learn everything they could about their family histories and their grandparents' lives. Those elders were happy to talk about their hard lives and the small beauties that made those lives bearable. The students began to get a sense of the value of their place in the world.[2] It was an excellent idea and the result is a set of books that is still eagerly collected and pored over.

There is a center there now, in Mountain City, Georgia, where artists and scholars come to learn these old ways. The Foxfire Museum and Heritage Center continues the work of those students, giving modern generations of Appalachian students a chance to understand the importance of the region and their place in it.

At the turn of the last century, before those unruly students badgered their grandmas about canning and their great-uncles about smithcraft, visitors to the Smoky Mountains were charmed by the old-fashioned way the people talked and were taken by the handicrafts their clever hands produced. They were also surprised and delighted to discover that many of the popular ballads could be traced back directly to Britain and Francis Child's splendid collection. The songs had been passed down mouth to ear since the earliest migrations from that land to this.

~~~~~~

2. Eliot Wigginton, ed., Foxfire, 12 vols. (New York: Anchor Books, 1972–2004).

These people came to be called "songcatchers." John C. Campbell was one of several "reformers" who came into the southern highlands at the turn of the twentieth century. Concerned with the lack of education and the level of perceived poverty, these missionaries toured the area, talking to farmers about their farming methods and their lives. Campbell was recently married to Olive Dame, a folklorist, and they traveled together—he interviewing, she listening to ballads and tales. Campbell died in 1919, and Olive and her companion Marguerite Butler spent months visiting the folk high schools that flourished in Scandinavia. They returned to Brasstown, North Carolina, where they established a folk school, which they named after Campbell. The John C. Campbell Folk School survives to this day and does a brisk summer program of handicraft classes and arts programming.

The Campbells' missionary zeal to better the lives of mountain people was clear, but some of the people who came into the region—before and after—cared only about what could be carried away. The Tennessee Valley Authority was formed to dam rivers to create lakes for recreation and tourism and for hydroelectric power for what's called "rural electrification." This began opening up the region to the scrutiny of a largely judgmental wider community.

When I spoke at that Harvard colloquium all those years ago, I quipped that I was everyone's worst fear: an educated redneck. I was the first in my family to graduate from high school, went on to university, and, ultimately, achieved the highest degree then available in my field. That means I walk in several worlds and code-switch when I need to. I am a liminal woman who has got above her raising, neither the one thing nor the other but both and neither. I attend festivals and conferences hundreds of miles from home and talk endlessly about my beautiful broken culture. And I stay here, a few miles from the cove where I grew up, living in the same neighborhood near the old river that my great-grandparents moved into at the end of the nineteenth century. This old mill village has seen worse days, for now it is gentrified and in-filled, with the original mill housing tarted up and selling for shocking amounts of money.

One midsummer day I sat with two women from West Virginia, and we talked through some of these hard issues. Remember when mountain people prided themselves on their self-sufficiency? mused one. On their independence? When we had gumption, the other one said. Gumption, we repeat, nodding. Yes.

The old witches had gathered in the shade. We had finished a corn dolly class that included an informative talk about corn and all it does and is. We had a quick supper and soon settled into some good talk about balm of Gilead, goose grease, and the present status of Appalachia.

These two women are beautiful in a peculiarly mountain way. Clear skin, strong features, a deliberate eye. Their hands told of lives of work, but the nails were manicured and perfect. The smiles of Appalachian women are like a light coming on in the darkness, and you are fortunate to have one bestowed upon you.

What is wrong here, with our people? With us? I've written elsewhere about the ragged wound that plagues so much of the region and seems to fester more day by sad day. It's economic, to be sure. No good jobs—not many jobs at all. People are scared and angry. Mining was good money at its peak, union labor in a lot of places. A man could do for his family, even if he ended his days too soon, with ruined lungs. The company took care of widows and orphans, and sons proudly followed their daddies underground. Every little company-owned house had a garden and the children had new shoes and good clothes. Money could be put back for a rainy day or a sick child or a ruined alcoholic relative.

Oxy. Meth. Heroin. Heroin laced with fentanyl. That's the sequence of the drug invasions, according to the sisters. We recalled the 2013 documentary *Oxyana* and laughed bitterly to remember the days when we only worried about oxycodone. Now, of course, we know that oxycodone was an intentional scourge on people deemed unimportant, smallpox blankets for poor white people.

The deeper we dig into the various cause-and-effect streams that are modern Appalachia, the more likely we are to find an obvious point that is as true now as it was in the time of the Native removals. No group outside the region is likely to have the people and the land here as their first priority. As federal- and state-sanctioned pipelines burst through homesteads and forests, the people who live in those places have little or no agency as the wreckage breaks all around them. Companies set to frack a potentially gas-rich region are impervious to culture or land ownership. Eminent domain has always been an implacable process, rarely fought successfully, often bankrupting the property owners with lawyer and court fees long before a trial can run its course. And even when it doesn't fall short, the damage is inflicted elsewhere—upon neighbors and forests and townships. When yet another mining company declares bankruptcy as the seams run out, to avoid pension and medical care payments, we must learn once again to rely on each other, to learn from each other and to have each other's backs. When disaster strikes, we all decided, it is the people on the ground—those most deeply affected—who are often the first of the first responders. Our legendary self-reliance must come out of whatever closet we've left it in as we deal with the realities of modern American life. Relearning old skills is on the minds—and schedules—of many worried Americans. And it hasn't been that long since the people of Appalachia knew a thing or two about making do and surviving in hard times.

And about magic, though that word is not so often used. This area has been settled by many people over its very long history. The nomadic Woodland-era folks came and went, as did DeSoto, Juan Pardo, and the other conquistadors, questing for gold for their Catholic majesties in Spain. So many tribal people here—to-ing and fro-ing, conquering and retreating—that it's hard to name them all. Here in my little corner of the southern highlands, the land knew the Shawnee, the Creek, and of course the Cherokee. When my ancestors came, they brought with them their strict religion along with the well of custom and folk belief that color my life down to this very day.

Protestants. No frills, Nicene Creed Protestants. Baptists, Methodists, Presbyterians, Church of God. KJV Bible believers who had a strange fatalism about life, understanding that whatever was endured in the earthly realm gave you stars on your crown in heaven. My grandfather (technically, my step-grandfather but the only grandfather I had ever known) was a Methodist lay minister and a kindhearted man. He held an old-fashioned vision of the afterlife. In his heaven, there were pearl-encrusted gates, streets paved with gold, and the longed-for ability to play the harp. He had never been musically inclined, but he loved music and looked forward to his own seat in the heavenly orchestra. I know he is there, right now, plucking strings that never have to be tuned or changed.

These European immigrants brought healing techniques with them from their country of origin, and they understood healing in a broad sense that included healing the spirit and mending broken hearts as well as broken relationships. That sort of healing is my study as well as my practice, and I apply the word *healing* to many kinds of work in many situations. I generally don't refer to myself as a healer because that feels bold and forward to me, and this work must always be done with humility and a sense of gratitude to the Greater Powers from whom the ability flows. We are merely vessels and messengers. I had a great-aunt who could remove warts. She was one of my grandmother's older sisters and was admirably humble. She died before I was born, but I understand the treatment went something like this: You and your warts came to sit beside her, and she welcomed you with her soft voice. (My mother's family were mostly soft-spoken but I understand my father's family—especially the women—were blessed with sharp tongues and powerful lungs.) My great-aunt would lightly touch the bewarted place, rubbing it with her thumb. The whole time she'd be looking you right in the eye and murmuring, "I don't know why folks come to me for this. I don't have any skill at all. How is your mama doing? You give her a big old hug from me, won't you, sugar?" The warts would fall off about three days later. But she never took credit. She had no skill in the matter and certainly no authority over warts.

Some of these folkways seem to be passed down through families by the family members who are the keepers of the collected lore. These are the oral histories that sometimes get broken in these years of far-flung families and of children who don't have much interest in those old superstitious ways. This happened with the father of my best friend in high school. Only a few years ago this talented musician and scalawag asked me if I could tell him something. He was, he continued, the seventh son of a seventh son. I probably gasped because that is as near Appalachian royalty as I am ever likely to get. What am I supposed to know? he asked. My heart sank. I don't know. Didn't your daddy tell you? He shook his shaggy old head. He tried to, he said. But all I wanted to do was drink liquor and play music. He was an accomplished musician, playing professionally for much of his adult life. And he didn't have seven sons so that he could pass the knowledge in the traditional fashion. He did have two sons and could've passed it on to them, not following the exact letter of the law. But it might not have worked even with the compromise. In any case, those skills and knowledge would have passed on with him when he left us only a few years later.

Oral traditions depend on several things. They must be shared. They must be heard. And they must be remembered. All of which run in a cycle throughout generations. When the line is broken—for whatever reason—that piece of the puzzle, that strand in the weaving, is lost for all time. In the long history of humankind on the planet, it is heartbreaking to think what has been lost through inattention, migration, war, and genocide. Most of it was probably simple things that made life a little easier or helped with birth or comforted the grieving.

The Ulster-Scots

Wart removal and blood binding and whatever we've lost—many of these things seem to come in batches to the people here who are of Scots-Irish descent. Also called the Scotch-Irish or the Ulster-Scots, these folks have a fascinating history that begins in the borderlands between Scotland and England. I grew up assured that part of my ancestry was Scots-Irish and that's what made us proud and fierce, though no one in my family had possessed a nice lilting brogue for centuries. It was a given for many of us and I didn't think much about it.

The Scots-Irish have been the subject of many books and films and among their numbers are the illustrious as well as the infamous:

Andrew Jackson, Bill Clinton, Davy Crockett, June Carter Cash, Johnny Cash, Carrie Fisher, Martha Graham, Anjelica Huston, Dolly Parton, Edgar Allan Poe, Neil Armstrong, Rosa Parks, and Barack Obama.

Then I was introduced (or perhaps reintroduced) to a group of people known variously as the Border Reivers, the Moss Helmets, and the Steel Bonnets. How did I ever learn about them? What books or movie highlighted their escapades, those pirates on ponies?

They lived—and some still do—on the Anglo-Scots borders. When the two kingdoms skirmished into and out of each other's homelands, the families in the border regions were always the first line of defense. Difficult to create and sustain a regular economy or a peaceful way of life when you were never safe from attack. These families lived as many tribal people, including their Gael ancestors, had: by raiding. *Riding* it was and is called, and if you say the two words back-to-back several times you'll realize it's the same word spoken with different dialects. Much of the old Reivers culture is robust, even to this day, though the raiding parties are largely symbolic, as far as I know.

The families along the border trusted neither state nor religious authority. They looked to the clan chieftain or the head of their extended family for wisdom. They were suspicious of outsiders, passionate, and quick to anger. We have records of their heart-rending ballads, courtesy of Sir Walter Scott. All those pieces came together for me to form a portrait of family and friends here in the mountains.

When James VI of Scotland became James I of the United Kingdom, one of the first things that everyone could agree on was that someone in authority needed to clear the lawless northern marches. (A march, by the way, is a border between realms, governed by a marquess or marquise.) With the union of the two kingdoms the word itself had to go and those areas became "shires." The other thing that had to go were the Border Reivers. Some were rounded up and killed outright. Others became mercenaries on the continent. Some hid out in the rough country and lived to fight another day.

And a great chunk of them were picked up by their scruffy necks and transported into Ulster. In their excellent book *From Ulster to Carolina: The Migration of the Scotch-Irish to Southwestern North Carolina*, H. Tyler Blethen and Curtis W. Wood Jr. recount the rest of the story.[3] The migration from Ulster through the Port of Philadelphia and down into the southern highlands of this old mountain chain is one of the foundation stones of the Appalachian story. But only one. I must reiterate that this is a region of many different cultures that have sometimes coexisted peacefully and sometimes not. To impose on it a sort of monolithic wash is to deny the various flavors a chance to be tasted on their own.

In their wonderful book *Wayfaring Strangers: The Musical Voyage from Scotland and Ulster to Appalachia*, Fiona Ritchie and Doug Orr trace the journey of my people through the music that survives on both sides of the Atlantic. Early in the twentieth century, missionaries to the region (like the Campbells) were charmed by the music here, which seemed eerily familiar. These songcatchers tracked many of these old ballads back to the British Isles and Ireland. These ragged immigrants carried a remarkable cache of folkways with them to their new home—music, medicine, magic—that

3. H. Tyler Blethen and Curtis W. Wood, *From Ulster to Carolina: The Migration of the Scotch-Irish to Southwestern North Carolina* (Raleigh: North Carolina Division of Archives and History, 1998).

are still a vital part of Appalachian life.[4] These aren't the only influences, of course. But they are the ones that we will explore in the coming pages since they are the ones I know best.

For my purposes—and the purposes of this book—I will focus on my own flavor of this Appalachian buffet, the piece of it that claims me (at least partially) and the piece I know best. But I will happily sprinkle what I know of all the other flavors so you can have a taste of them.

I have a confession to make. It is one I have made before, so don't clutch your pearls just yet. When I first started writing about and teaching these folkways, I was holding on to a fear that the modern world would soon smother these strange old ways. My work seemed to be to record them before they were lost. But I soon discovered these folkways are still being practiced by folks who learned them from family members or neighbors. Any time I get down to talking about this with people like me, whose families have lived in the region for many generations, I discover a new story or a new cure or a variation on something I already know. Like our Border Reiver ancestors, we have learned to be closed-mouthed with strangers until we feel safe.

Several years ago, I spoke at a small Baptist college about twenty minutes north of me. It was a women in religion class, and I was speaking about the resurgence of goddess worship, especially among feminists. I spoke my piece to a quiet group that took a few notes. The professor then asked me a question about my folk magic practice.

Now there was a group of stern young men seated on my left down the long table. They neither looked at me nor spoke to me

---

4. Fiona Ritchie and Doug Orr, *Wayfaring Strangers: The Musical Voyage from Scotland and Ulster to Appalachia* (Chapel Hill: University of North Carolina Press, 2014).

until I began talking about cures, interesting and useful native plants, and my kinfolk. Those young men perked right up then and sat up. The allotted class time came to an end and the right-hand side of the table quickly decamped, checking their phones. The young silent fellows jumped up and surrounded me as I rose to leave. They told me about their grandmas and aunties and all the things they did that was exactly as I described. We talked there for about twenty minutes and as they left several of them shook my hand. Though I don't know it for sure, I suspect some of them went home to tell their grandma or auntie about the woman from Asheville that talked in their class. And I fancy a couple of them were the first college students in their families, as I was.

As I ramble around the Appalachian hills and wander farther afield in my work as teacher and preacher, I marvel at all the pieces of history and culture that weave together to form this place. With new influences coming in all the time, the southern highlands are a place where there are many flavors, flavors that somehow blend together to enhance the whole.

Some Witchery: Appalachian Meditation

Stilling the noise all around us so that we may rest or think deeply is a common problem in our over-caffeinated world. Many of us have tried Eastern styles of meditation and found them difficult to master to the point of being useable. A walking meditation is a good way to clear your head and get some gentle exercise. This only requires that you walk in a place where you don't have to be mindful of traffic, where you can let your mind wander.

On those days when walking isn't possible, consider a candle meditation. Make yourself a cup of whatever warming beverage you prefer. Take your drink to a quiet place, whether porch or kitchen or backyard. Light a candle of any size and color and sit in front of it. Take time drinking your drink and as you sip it, simply look at the candle. That's all. And here's what is likely to happen: I recommend you do this for seven days in a row to master the technique. For the first few days, your thoughts will jump around, and it will be difficult to look at the little flame. After that, you'll find that the thoughts that are jumbling your mind will fall to the bottom and the things you want to consider (whether it's solving a problem or coming up with a new idea) will stay present in the front of your mind. A couple more days of this practice will focus those present and helpful thoughts and the time will seem to pass much more quickly.

This is a good way to start your day or something to consider adding to your bedtime routine, especially if you are looking to practice more lucid dreaming. It is also a way to settle your nerves after a shock and to bring your mind and your body into better communication.

Chapter 2

Betwixt, the Ineffable
Magic of Place

These hills march their old, shaggy selves into the past as well as the present, sometimes loping a bit into the future. Those gentle slopes belie their deep history, and any who choose to engage in the energy of the place would do well to remember that time moves differently here. In my work in the spirit realms, I fancy it is easier in this time-muffled place, where we are often betwixt and between, neither here nor there.

This old land is filled with liminal places and gives rise to ballads and tales. In these pages we will work through our harsh and complicated history on the strings of a fiddle, in the stitches of a quilt made of scraps, and with words on paper. Each one of us as liminal as a hedgerow with complicated histories and tattered souls.

I am an urban homesteader, a gardener, a subsistence farmer, and what old-timers would have called a "good eater." Not many processed foods but an omnivore's full range of dietary choices. When my vegetarian and vegan friends quip about eating anything with a face, I like to remind them that I have raised chickens and I have raised broccoli. Broccoli is at least as sentient as chickens. It just isn't mobile. That is certainly my observation of the natural world, and it invites us to consider our relationship with and within that world. The Native Americans here (the Shawnee, Creek, and Cherokee, to name a few whose names we know) knew their place in the web of all being, and that place was not superior to the biosphere that sustained them, their homeland.

The arrival of nominally Christian settlers changed the landscape, literally and figuratively. That is when Genesis reared its ugly head, with its message of domination over nature, its order to subdue nature and control it. The language of domination—along with the self-serving doctrine of Manifest Destiny—that gets lifted from the Genesis creation myth cycle has been one of the most destructive forces in the human-habitat interaction. We are to master the land, to subdue it, to bend it to our will.

It may be hard to understand the love we have for these places, even as we allow their destruction to continue. To feel the grip of the land beneath your feet, you need to cultivate a relationship to it. Forgive my chauvinism as I relate tales of this old land, and please don't take offense. For all the land is connected just as all of everything is: the mountains are in friendship with the seas and the desert is in love with the high prairie. As with all in nature, this gives humans an opportunity to invoke the overused notion of interdependence. We read that word in all sorts of places, but I continue to see it expressed as an acknowledgment of one group's perceived superiority in the face of the Other. Interdependence is actually about our common vulnerabilities, not one group's ability to "save" its less fortunate, and therefore lesser, neighbors. Appalachian people used to know this and are now in the painful process of relearning it.

One of the most dynamic and destructive divides in the nation is the rural-urban one. It catches us economically, politically, and spiritually. We get locked into it in ways that make no sense at all. When we look at the perception of the Appalachian region from the outside, we see the struggle writ large, and we see how it drives concepts of compassion and mercy for people who patently don't deserve it. The despised stereotypes are rooted in older stories of estrangement, war, and migration. European migrants arrived in the fastnesses of the southern highlands bound on finding lives of solitude and noninterference. This is reflected in the dark splendor of Protestant Christianity as it was and is practiced here. It is embedded in the music and song we relish.

Extraction

In our hearts, we always return to this land that has nurtured, sheltered, and hidden us, from which we have extracted livelihood and dubious safety. To understand us and to ponder our ties to this homeplace is to bide with the concept of extraction and all it has done to the land and the people in it.

The point is that extraction—the cultural strip-mining—removes something and often puts nothing else in the empty space. The sad history of colonialism has shown us again and again what profound effects extraction has on the land and the people on it. Blood diamonds are one example of global awareness of a particularly heinous extraction industry in Africa.

In Appalachia, I suppose you could say the curse of extraction began with the forced Indian removals, what we have come to call the Trail of Tears. The Cherokee, Muscogee/Creek, Chickasaw, Seminole, and Choctaw were driven out of their ancestral lands and force-marched to Oklahoma. The removals were done with the same level of cruelty that we have come to expect from empires. There was no pretense of equipping the people, no pretense about acknowledging their humanity. We are still unsure of the exact number of deaths, but some official reports claim ten thousand died of hunger, cold, and disease before the remaining people reached the Indian Territory in Oklahoma.[5] They were extracted, removed, though some hid out in the laurel hells and caves later to reorganize as the Eastern Band of Cherokee Indians. Those who survived the twenty-two hundred mile trek became the Cherokee Nation at Tahlequah. Those unaffiliated and unregistered—not on the official rolls—call themselves the Free Cherokee. My friend David's father was nearly fully Cherokee, but he and his son chose to make their way in the world without relying on government grace or tribal mercy. David married Connie, a descendant of Daniel Boone, in an interesting but hardly unusual pairing.

After the removal, the forest extraction began in earnest. The story of Appalachia is, in part, the story of extraction industries moving into the region, taking away natural resources, and leaving the land naked and broken. The woodlands were clear-cut twice, leaving small patches of so-called virgin forest in hard-to-log places. Joyce Kilmer Memorial Forest on Little Santeetlah Creek has been protected since 1936.[6] Almost four thousand acres of old-growth forest were protected by that designation, and the forest contains some stunning examples of woodland elders: straight-sided tulip poplars eighty feet tall, cucumber trees (*Magnolia acuminata*), and those strangely magical beeches that grow on the trunks of their silvered dead. To walk the figure eight trail at Joyce

5. Gregory Smithers, *Native Southerners: Indigenous History from Origins to Removal* (Norman, OK: University of Oklahoma Press, 2019).

6. "Joyce Kilmer Memorial Forest," USDA Forest Service, accessed August 4, 2020, www.fs.usda.gov/recarea/nfsnc/recarea/?recid=48920.

Kilmer is to find yourself among literal giants, beings that have reached their two- or three- or four-century span simply because the terrain was too difficult or expensive to log. There are other forests in the region as "ancient as the hills" as the poet says, but the Joyce Kilmer Memorial Forest is protected and accessible for now.[7]

So the forests went first. As we look at the extraction industries that continue to do their damage in the greater region, it makes sense to begin with the logging that was omnipresent in the southern highlands, beginning in the eighteenth century. But the industrial exploitation got a grip in the region at the end of the nineteenth century.

Author and outdoorsman Horace Kephart was an early fan of the region, coming here to live early in the twentieth century and writing about the region and woodcraft. One of his best-known books is *Our Southern Highlanders*. His understanding of the devastation of extraction industries came from his experience in the region and his interviews with the people responsible. He wrote, "A northern lumberman admitted to me, with frankness unusual in his class, that 'All we want here is to get the most we can out of the country, as quick as we can, and then get out.'"[8] In 1925, Kephart wrote, "Everyone who has seen the havoc and desolation the lumberman leaves in his wake knows how inexpressibly sad he is as he turns and flees from the sight of it."[9]

7. Samuel Taylor Coleridge, "Kubla Khan," Poetry Foundation, 1816, https://www.poetryfoundation.org/poems/43991/kubla-khan.

8. Horace Kephart, *Our Southern Highlanders: A Narrative of Adventure in the Southern Appalachians and a Study of Life among Mountaineers* (New York: Outing Publishing, 1913), 357.

9. Horace Kephart, "The Smoky Mountain National Park," *The High School Journal* 8, no. 6/7 (1925): 64.

Coal was next, of course. The rich coal land of Kentucky, West Virginia, and other states brought good jobs, ways for men to support their families, more reliable than subsistence farming. "Jobs" is one of many battle cries of Appalachian culture. The world that grew up around coal—and to a certain extent the mill culture that followed it—was the perfect storm of ecological carelessness, human greed, and unfettered capitalism.

The coal seams were picked out and hauled away. When the profits lessened, the companies began clear-cutting the new forests in order to scrape off the thin topsoil with earth-moving machinery and then to take the coal. Mountaintop removal was the next logical step as whole mountains were blasted away, minerals extracted, and detritus dumped into the waterways, changing the shape and texture of the region. Fracking is the latest insult and the desecration of pipelines (as well as potential pipeline breaks with their subsequent terrible spills) to bring the gas from the fracking fields to the ports is palpable. Again the landscape is slashed and roadways for pipelines replace the wild variety of medicinal plants and wild foodstuff and the homes of long-time residents are flattened in the name of progress.

Next came the Civil War with its loss of life and its complicated tale of divided loyalties. Many mountain families remained staunchly loyal to the Union, in spite of their geographic placement. My Ballard family's odd Civil War drama (as I understand one of the family myths) includes an ancestor who joined the Confederate States of America only to be disappointed in the poor quality of the food on offer. I believe he defected somewhere in Tennessee, and I have no recollection of how he was received upon his return, if he did, in fact, return.

The story of my mother's family comes down in a little more detail. Growing up, I heard that my part of the family had come to Haywood County from South Carolina because great-great-grandpa was "shot by a Yankee." My curiosity got the better of me and I did some digging. It was near the end of the conflict when the Union sent William Sherman and others into the heart of the Confederate States to starve the people into submission. Sherman's Bummers were a group of largely lawless foragers, shock troops who rode through the South, often burning what they couldn't steal. Near Travelers Rest, South Carolina, a group of them took the family's plow horse, and my ancestor went after them, attempting to retain the use of the horse for the spring planting, swearing he'd find them and return the animal afterward. My ancestor was shot in the arm and returned home, horseless. He died three weeks later of sepsis. When my niece got sepsis last year, my mind went directly back to that long ago relation whose death drove the women of the family north into the mountains, presumably to make a new home with distant relatives there.

It lingers with some families, even up here in the mountains where we were sometimes unsure of where our allegiance should fall. I remember walking with a friend from Texas (by way of Maine) near the Battery in Charleston. She passed yet another street plaque and, in a frustrated voice, she demanded to know why the South couldn't let it go. After all, the war was long over and the South, she said, her voice rising in pitch, had *lost*. I smiled at her and squeezed her arm, then quietly told her about the plow horse and the drawn-out painful death. She got thoughtful. When did your people come to America? I asked. The 1930s, she replied. They fled Nazi Germany. I nodded. For many families in the South, the story is one of death, of deprivation, and sometimes of renewal. We carry our family tales—whether they are entirely true or not—like heavy strongboxes, easily opened. If there could have been a truth and reconciliation commission here, like the ones in South

Africa following apartheid, it might have been different. If Reconstruction had been handled better, it might have been different. But the South was never fully reintegrated into the Union, and that plagues the republic down to this very day.

The next extraction in my part of the mountains was the industrialized timber industry. Most of the southern forests were clear-cut at this time. The glory of those forests was the American chestnut tree—*Castanea dentata*. It was an extraordinary tree, enormous and fast growing, reaching almost one hundred feet high and ten feet in diameter. A blight arrived in the United States on imported chestnut trees at the beginning of the twentieth century, and by the Roaring Twenties, it had killed upward of three billion trees. *Castanea dentata* is rarely seen as an adult specimen in its former range, though the American Chestnut Foundation is working earnestly to develop a successful hybrid and is having slow and steady success with its quest.

It towered above most of the hardwoods, and its girth made it a prize for furniture and home building. I can't overemphasize the importance of this tree to the ecosystems of the ancient forests. They were logged indiscriminately before the destructive blight did its damage. Logging provided lucrative but dangerous jobs for lightly educated mountain men. Camps were set up throughout the region and the men sent money home to their families, what money they didn't owe to the company store, as well as money spent on alcohol and the inevitable sex workers who attached themselves to the camps.

My neighbor Beecher was pretty old when we moved in beside the house where he lived with his wife Pearl in the 1980s. He worked in the logging camps of Haywood County when he was a young man and loved to tell us stories about it. He was a friendly character and shockingly brave. We watched him rig a scaffolding on his roof so he could replace his shingles. He was in his eighties then and did the job alone, not asking for or accepting help. It was the kind of self-sufficiency that used to be common in the area but has fallen out of favor in these urban-focused times.

One of my prized possessions is a short stack of chestnut planks given to me by my grandmother. They are wormy chestnut and painted green. *Wormy chestnut* is the descriptive name for lumber sawn from chestnut trees that died from the blight and continued to stand, and feeding insects give it its distinctive wormy appearance. These inherited planks served as bookshelves at my grandmother's earlier house, and she had them stored in her garage until she decided what she wanted done with them. They are stored on my porch and will soon resume their shelf duties. I will hold them dear, as a remnant of a time that is long past and a tree we may never see thriving here again.

As we continued to cut down these great trees, to destroy the ecosystem built around them, the southern forests were hit by a series of devastating plant diseases. The chestnut blight was not the first, but its effect was profound. It is with us still, this fungus. Its name is *Cryphonectria parasitica*. It has never, not down to the present day, been eradicated, nor has a cure been found for it. There are still chestnut trees in the southern highlands, but they barely reach a breedable age before the fungus strikes. They continue on for a few years but they rarely thrive, never again to become the giants of former days. We kept cutting and killing these trees, harvesting in an unstoppable cycle, a cycle that continued until nature found a way to stop it. When I am feeling fanciful, I consider the notion that we kept removing them subconsciously proving that they were unneeded and unwanted. And so they went, leaving our forests bereft, an allegory of our sad extractive history.

Soil, Forest, Mast, Magic

With so much taken away from so small a place, one might think that the spirit of the place might feel diminished, less than it had once been. The height of the mountains belies the power here. The old rivers—the New River, the French Broad, the Nolichucky (lovingly called the Chuck)—are not so broad or fast as the Ohio or the Mississippi. It is tempting to dismiss them as small and unimportant, but you'd be mistaken. During the regular heavy downpours of this temperate rain forest, the waters often rise up into the floodplains where the careless or unaware have built homes and businesses then settle back into their modest beds.

In my spiritual tradition, we talk about a "veil" between the worlds of matter and spirit. We know the power of liminal spaces, of being neither here nor there but betwixt the two. When you are betwixt, you have a foot in both worlds and can move from one to the other. The betwixt place is tempting because it is terribly interesting and terribly powerful and we don't exactly know the rules there. It is the magic of liminality, of the hedge, of the place that is neither the one thing nor the other.

In walking that wobbly line between magic and the everyday, I realized there isn't a firm boundary between the two places. I've begun asking festivalgoers to stop referring to their daily lives as "mundane" or "mundania" in order re-enchant their everyday lives and the world around them. I gently remind them that people have been practicing all this witchery for generations and practicing it where they live, not saving it up for a special weekend with coreligionists. The work that puts beans on your table may be bank teller, but there's no reason why that can't be infused with magic and intention. In fact, I refer to any act of folk magic as work or a job of work. I don't know if that is traditional or if I read it somewhere, but the fact of the matter is I've called it that for so long that it has stuck like a burr. I have a little black case that my daughter gave me, and when I pack it for an energy clearing or to do a bit of ghost-busting, I pat its nubby surface and mutter, "Time for a little job of work." Our small acts of re-enchantment may improve our attitude, our practice, and the lives of the people (and other beings) we encounter every day. It isn't necessary to wear special jewelry or a particular outfit in order to do this work that is so wrapped up in our natural world.

In pondering the concept of this spirit of place—of all things and beings ensouled, each of us rambling betwixt the worlds of matter and spirit—I sat in my yard and looked around. Everything in my view had a soul, to my way of thinking, and was sentient in its own way. My eye caught a few things that felt like they were leaning in, to tell me more, or maybe to listen in.

There is magic inherent in soil, forest, and mast. My thoughts went from one to another and I found myself straightening my back and listening intently, as though feeling my way to some place I didn't quite know.

Soil

There is a little planting bed beside the front steps near the gate. It gets no sun at all during most of the day but gets blasted all summer long with the baking afternoon sun. In the spring it holds hyacinths, tulips, and grape hyacinths, but it's usually a sorry naked place in the summer and fall. A couple of weeks ago my husband, the champion composter, added in some homemade soil and moved a couple of runaways into that bed. The runaways included a scented flowering tobacco that was growing in a crack in the concrete walk and another mystery plant he'd been given by one of his gardening buddies. I added a black-eyed Susan I saved from a house in our neighborhood that is due for demolition. We've been religious about watering the planting bed, and every time I do, I breathe in the fragrance of that young soil.

Soil is tiny bits of stone, with rotted leaves and sticks tossed in, carcasses of insects and small mammals, with enough water and heat to make it friable. It passes through the gut of innumerable earthworms and those castings also become soil. Even a poor soil consists of this extraordinary alchemical potion, made up of so many tangible pieces of the organic world.

Soil comes in many densities and combinations of materials. Much of the southern highlands of Appalachia are covered with a thin layer of soil, which is true of many forested mountain areas. This layer is easily destroyed through clear-cutting and other careless logging, which causes that skinny layer to flow down the sides of the hills, often clogging streams and branches below.

The most prized soil is called "bottom land" and is found in the floodplains of creeks and rivers. This soil is deep and rich, as it benefits from the occasional flooding of the river. It also has the distinct advantage of being flat and more easily tilled, planted, and tended. With the advent of toxic farm runoff and chemicals freely dumped in local waterways, this soil (like all soils) should be tested, not only for nutrients or deficiencies but also for heavy metals and other toxic residue.

Much of the soil here contains a generous amount of clay, which helps retain moisture in times of drought but is heavy going for the roots of tender plants. The opposite may also be found: sandy soil that doesn't hold water but is easy for plant roots to move through. Most serious gardeners will find a balance of moisture retention and friability through building up their soil by adding composted plant material.

Forest

The wretched and destructive squirrels demand my attention, racing up and down the big maples. I observe them and remember the trees in the woods across the river. I was raised in the woods and used to know my way through those trees, walking easily and confidently. When I was growing up, the times seemed safer than now, and I would leave my house on a sunny morning and return hours later, having wandered far and seen much. My daughter was raised years later in an urban setting but she still holds some woodland skills and some common sense I am unreasonably proud of that.

Consider the magic inherent in the forests of the world, magic that comes down to us through folk and fairy tales. There is always more to the forest than meets the eye. From the canopy above to the mycelium layer in the soil, there are so many things unseen, so many possibilities for magic and danger.

I returned to the woods after a long absence—an absence in which I left rural life, launched a career in the arts, married, and had a child. In all that time, I busied myself with new ways (and flush toilets!) and hardly missed the world I called home for so many formative years.

Then a friend invited me for a walk in a wooded park nearby. He pointed out the plants he knew so well and we marveled over the young trees, including a scraggly American chestnut. The area had been clear-cut and then used as a dump by the county. It had been left to lie for many years and the city traded something for it in order to create a city park in that neighborhood. The fast-growing but short-lived trees—the pines—zoomed up, providing some cover for all the rest. But first came the briars, poison ivy, and Virginia creeper because humans had done so much damage and these plants are always the first responders in passive restoration. Consider the natural magic of this protective covering and how we as humans utilize prickles and energetic poison to cover and protect ourselves and others when the need arises.

Mast

In old Appalachia, the people predicted the severity of the upcoming winter with beans and mast. Mast is the output of wild trees—acorns and nuts, mostly. A heavy mast year indicates a winter of colder than usual temperatures, snow, and ice. It foretells a winter in which the wild things will need extra feeding supplies. We know from history that this mast also served to feed the people who lived here long ago, as well as the new crop of primitive skills aficionados.

What We Are

A friend asked if I'd ever seen the 2010 movie *Winter's Bone*. Indeed, yes. In fact when people outside the region ask me what life is like here—to be of here with these gnarly roots—I usually ask the same question. Appalachia has been so mythologized over the years that we lie somewhere between quaint throwbacks to Elizabethan England and the urbanoia of *Deliverance*. But the reality of Appalachian people, as you have come to discover, is that we are not a monolith, and for some of us the truth of our real lives is nearer *Winter's Bone* than either of the other extremes. Neither Andy of Mayberry nor Jed Clampett—and yet all of these too. The ideas compacted into the hillbilly stereotypes need some freedom, as well as an open mind, to receive the unpacking of them and to allow real lives to show their true selves.

Winter's Bone clearly holds up three aspects of Appalachian culture that are important for outsiders to know and indwellers to acknowledge—family, making do, and fatalism. We'll unpack each one and weave them as we can into our understanding of the region and its inhabitants. Then we'll move on to the spirit folk who also lay claim to the region.

When the Border Reivers were removed into Ulster in the seventeenth century, they were justly notorious for several things. Due to generations of living in a war zone between two powerful nations, they rode throughout the borderlands on swift, silent ponies, stealing sheep, cattle, and most anything that wasn't nailed down. They lived, so we understand as their Gael ancestors had lived. They were Scottish and English, with bits and bobs from different Continental sources, making this group one of the most genetically diverse in western Europe.

These unusual circumstances made the borderers suspicious of any authority, secular or religious. Trust was placed in the head of the family and then the chieftain of their particular clan. Their general mistrust of law and their prevalence in the southern highlands helps open a piece of the pervasive stereotype—the adherence to the family view and loyalty to the extended family. We are often said to be suspicious of strangers. Even if we do offer hospitality, there's rarely an extension of recognizable trust. When I was growing up, the sheriff's department (the law or the law-dogs) was rarely brought in, even for outrageous offences. Some reasons include the need to refrain from airing the family's dirty laundry in public because it is shameful, and the trope of not bringing outsiders in, not even potentially neutral ones, because they might discover things best left undiscovered. I track this to the Border

Reivers so long ago, scraping out a living in a place with little safety and no peace.

The question of trust—and even the ability to trust—looms large in Appalachia. Understandable given the way some people have been cheated out of home or livelihood here, generation after generation. This continues today as representatives of fracking interests misrepresent their intentions to landowners throughout the area, or so I am told.

Making do with what you have is the motto of people living in multigenerational poverty and isolation. What it means in practical terms is hard work. Plowing, planting, tending, harvesting, preserving. Subsistence farming means growing and preserving enough food for your entire family with little or no access to stores. Children got new shoes when the burley came in and was sold. In these mountains, many families depended on their tobacco allotment as a cash crop to buy the things that couldn't be grown and made and to pay the taxes on the land. Allotments are a state-imposed control over the supplies of a particular product, aimed to keep the market moderately supplied in order to keep the prices high. Those supports were removed less than a decade ago, as American demand for tobacco decreased. Most of the big farms still growing are located in the central and eastern part of North Carolina, and there are other cash crops now. The notion that a family could survive without ready cash until it was time to pay the landlord or the taxes goes back to European peasantry. Here in the southern Appalachians, you ate what you grew, hunted, caught, or picked free off the land. Today we talk about "value-added" products, which is a fancy way of saying you picked and dried three herbs, combined them to create incense and put them in a jar with a label. Everything that could be used was used. Anything that could be eaten was eaten. It used to be said that every part of a slaughtered hog was used in some way, except for the tail and the squeal.

The strange magic of these strange places has a deep appeal now, as modern practitioners look for magic that is authentic, as well as magic that works. Often the seeds of that magic lie in the land under our feet and the rivers that flow through the land. The savvy practitioner will look to the land for strength as well as inspiration. To find the essence of your magical practice in the heart of nature is also an act of spiritual reclamation.

Some Witchery: Acquiring Good Luck

If you study magic workings through history, you may find, as I have, a curious thing: the idea of being lucky or of having good (or bad) luck used to be more prevalent than it seems to be in more recent writings and discussions. Charms and talismans to either improve one's luck or draw good luck to you used to be very popular. There are probably valid reasons why we don't consider the amount or quality of our personal luck as much as we used to.

In my work, I find that a return to the idea of improved luck is helpful for many of my friends and clients as they navigate through challenging times. I haven't encountered traditional Appalachian workings to improve your luck, though good luck has always been valued in the regional culture. There are many ways to ward off bad luck, like inscribing an X in the air when a black cat crosses your path. My family, being contrary, considered a black cat crossing to be a positive thing, but my grandmother was uneasy if a white cat did the same.

I created this job of work to improve your luck. It is cobbled together from traditional materials wielded in traditional ways.

But it is an invention of my own and not something I learned from a neighbor or family member.

We begin by embracing the idea that our natural state is lucky. That may require a change in your mindset and that may not be an easy thing if you've gone through your life this far thinking that luck never goes your way. Phrases like "just my luck" or "that figures" muttered after an unfortunate event imply that your expectation is that things won't go your way because you aren't a lucky so-and-so. Try replacing those with "lucky me" when something goes well and that will go a long way toward tweaking your attitude in the direction of a new outlook.

Begin by sweeping your home space from the front door to the back, leaving both doors open. Encourage air and new energy to flow through the area, blowing away bunged-up energy and old air. There are a few things to pull together: a pinch of dirt from your yard (or from a potted plant, if you don't have a yard), another pinch each of sour grass and catnip (fresh or dried), and some ground nutmeg. You'll also need some red thread and plain brown paper. Cut out a square of the paper, three inches by three inches or slightly larger. Embroidery floss is a good choice for thread. Use a felt-tipped pen to put a fat black dot in the middle of the paper and add the ingredients to the square. Stir them together with the first finger of your soft (nondominant) hand. Add something shiny to the mix—a sliver of mirror, a bit of foil, a chip of mica, or a little silver bead. Take that same finger and tap the top three times, thinking to yourself how lucky you are going to be from here on out.

Now fold that paper over on itself tight, so nothing falls out. Tie it up tight with the red string into a small package, a sachet. Tap it one more time, same as before, thinking the same things. Place that little sachet to your forehead, to your eyes, to your mouth, to your belly, and finally over your heart. Carry the sachet with you for at least seven days and nights, in your purse or your pocket. Lay it under a full moon as you can to keep it charged. Let your self-talk change to this: "My natural state is very lucky."

Chapter 3

Words, Music, and Magic

The generations of isolation took their toll, but they also left us something to fill the empty places. This is another piece that must also be considered whatever the culture: we are a tribe of storytellers, musicians, and mythmakers. A simple occasion becomes an entertainment or an object lesson that is then retold by one—or all—of the participants.

I refer to myself as a spellcatcher because one of the things that piques my curiosity is the roots of folk magic in southern Appalachia. It is a riff on the songcatchers that I mentioned in an earlier chapter. Many of my friends are music makers and it is a tradition that I grew up with. I grew up with a piano and took lessons for several years. I was never brilliant but I enjoyed playing—something I would still enjoy if I took the time to have the piano tuned. I have been teaching myself to play the fiddle, which has been as successful as my self-taught Irish-Gaelic (Gaeilge) studies, both of which would be more successful if I practiced. When I tell people where I'm from, they usually ask if I play music. I confess to these kind strangers that I am a terrible fiddler who longs to be mediocre. And when asked what I can play, I respond: scales, "Twinkle, Twinkle Little Star," "The Ashokan Farewell," and "Bonny Portmore."

Music plays such an important part in the lives of these mountains that it is hard to express how dear it is to us. It isn't just bluegrass and old-time music, of course. There is music everywhere here, in churches, on porches, in kitchens, and in picking parlors. We like to teach each other songs and tunes, and most circles will welcome new folks and encourage them to play along.

Many of these tunes came with the early settlers, and some were mostly forgotten in the place they began, the British Isles and Ireland. Cecil Sharp was one of the collectors who rediscovered them alive and well (and little altered) in the southern highlands of the Appalachians. His collection included enough versions of "Barbry Allen" to fill sixteen pages of his important book, *English Folk Songs of the Southern Appalachians*.[10]

These old songs and tunes are the roots of bluegrass and old-time music and still influence folk and country music down to this very day. They have been passed down in families and shared at festivals, each new generation adding its own flavor to this vital part of Appalachian culture. If you are ever fortunate enough to be asked to someone's porch on a warm summer evening for "music," you would do well to drop everything and get there. It will be a beautiful gift and something you'll remember for years to come.

Women's Work Songs as Incantation

As I've mentioned before, I have been most fortunate to visit the Alexander Carmichael Collection at the University of Edinburgh. Fortunate because I am beholden to Carmichael for his exten-

---

10. Cecil Sharp, *English Folk Songs of the Southern Appalachians* (Windsor, CT: Loomis House Press, 2012).

sive notes and for the publication of his *Carmina Gadelica*. It is a storehouse of riches, waiting to be retrieved by folks like me. On the occasion of the presentation of my first academic paper to the Appalachian Studies Association conference, a colleague mentioned that the traditional churning song, often called "Come, Butter, Come," was written up in *Carmina Gadelica*. The charm is common among the Deitsch communities in Pennsylvania and is well-known in Appalachia. It serves as both work song and magical working and is officially called "The Song of the Churn."

It harkens back to an earlier era where this—and other homely jobs—were a necessary part of rural life. Work done by women, mostly, and work that often includes a chant or song that does more than ease the burden of tedious work—the song was also an incantation for successful completion of the job at hand. The workers responsible were plentiful when I was a young woman in a rural part of the county, and their ranks include women on both my mother's side and my father's side of the family. You've maybe seen them too—wiry little women with hair that seems set like hoarfrost. Their hands are veiny, their knuckles large and bothersome. These are mountain women, hill women of indeterminate stock, the blood in their veins holding shadows of Britain and Africa, Germany and Native America. These mothers and aunties and grandmothers had little control over their reproductive lives and, as a result, many buried half the children they bore. There is rarely a record of miscarriages, and often the stillbirths were wept over and prayed over, then carried to the family's ridgetop burying ground and left to sleep, their final resting place marked only with a stack of pretty rocks, the only record of their non-lives seared on a weary mother's heart.

These women worked from before the sun rose until after night had fallen. They turned a dab hand to all domestic things, and as homesteaders like me try in vain to relearn the skills of their lifetimes, we appreciate their tenacity and strength, from cooking the daily meals and both growing and preserving the food that would see the household through lean months to doctoring the ills and accidents of living in a rural setting and catching babies up and down the cove. A cove where they may have lived their whole lives, going from their mother's house to the church house to their own little place with its plot of stony land.

These women, whom I am humbled to call my foremothers and elder cousins, have hearts like eagles, memories like elephants, and backs like oxen. They are scarce now as hen's teeth, and I want to remember and honor them by learning and teaching the work songs that punctuated the labor of their long days, starting with that churning song. You may have heard it, if you are a fan of regional folk music. There's so much old folklore connected with churning—how wicked spirits can steal the butter away from the cream and so forth—so this is a work song that is also a charm to ensure the arrival of sweet butter. It is rhythmic (as most work songs are) and keeps time with the up-and-down movement of the dasher in the churn.

This song, which I have tracked back to 1650, is interesting for a couple of reasons.[11] First, it has a long life and has traveled to many places with a few variants, all of which follow the same rhythmic patterns, of course.

Here's the most common version. It is simple and effective, repeated until the cream stiffens into butter:

---

11. Percy B. Green, "An Essex Charm for a Churn," in A History of Nursery Rhymes (London: Greening Co., 1899), 134, https://books.google.com/books /about/A_History_of_Nursery_Rhymes.html?id=-USFcfPEBe4C.

Churn, butter, churn!
Come, butter, come!
A little good butter
Is better than none.

A local variation mentions the source of the cream:

Come, butter, come!
Come, butter, come!
Cows in the pasture
Churn a little faster!
Come, butter, come!
Come, butter, come!

The other thing I especially appreciate about this work song is that it has internal variations depending on how long the churning will take. The words don't simply repeat, though they can if the churner wants to lose herself in thought while going through the repetitive motion. But imagine a novice churner, a young girl who is now set to do this job.

Come, butter, come; come, butter, come.
Daddy's standing at the gate
Waiting on his butter cake . . .

She can go on to everyone in the family (Granny, Georgie, Sissy), on to the neighbors (Missrus Bal, Preacher Dan), and from there to familiar Bible characters (Noah, Moses, Adam and Eve) to amuse herself until the job is done.

Connie Swafford of Candler, North Carolina, descendant of Daniel Boone and a multigeneration Appalachian woman, said this about her time at the churn: "It was mostly old hymns but was always something with a bump and swing to it." A bump and swing—some of the old hymns certainly have that. And the verses often hint at a hidden door to magic work.

I began to consider what sorts of chores were imposed and whether or not those could have some sort of rhythmic song attached to them. There is always plenty to do on a mountain smallholding and something for every size hand to do. Moving rocks out of the field and onto the edges was a child's job. Sitting in a straight-backed and cane-bottomed chair, peeling apples in the afternoon sunshine, was a granny's job. Whittling a toy for the babies was grandpa's job. And in between there was an endless array of things that needed to get done, probably last week. Snapping beans, weaving, spinning, hoeing, wood chopping, water drawing, washing, corn shucking, sweeping, hanging clothes on the line, plowing, milking—so many excuses to sing as we worked and to bring magic to the task at hand.

The Move into Towns

Appalachian women weren't only rural farm laborers. When many country people moved into the cities to find work, they stepped into the hellish world of Industrial Era mills. The villages that grew up around American mills had a sad similarity: small houses, larger ones for larger families, bathhouses, a clubhouse where unmarried men could hang out, and churches to get all those hardworking souls right with the Lord come Sunday. There were company stores, just like in mining towns. The mill owners paid as little as they could get away with, and whole families could be employed at the mill, from the age of six up. The work was dangerous, hard, and unrelenting, and a family could end up owing more to the company than could ever be paid off—in a tab to the store, the rent on their house, and any shortage in the pieces of work they were required to produce.

The work songs that have come out of these hard lives are rhythmic and sometimes poke fun at the bosses and other workers, sometimes express longing for the rural life they'd left behind. Like the farm songs, there were often many verses, and the rhythms varied according to the mill room in which the singers worked. Some of them included repetitious phrases designed to magically keep the singer and the other workers safe in a dangerous working environment, an example of which is a weave room song that features the repetitive phrase "I got the blues, I got the blues, I got them awful weave room blues."[12]

As more and more people move into the southern highlands, some are choosing to dive deeply into old and nearly lost ways of being in this old land, including the folkways and witchery. And time moves on, doesn't it? Grannies churned the butter. Their granddaughters worked in the mills. And *their* granddaughters? Working women are found in places that would have been unlikely even two generations ago. Where will the new songs and new spells come from, the ones Appalachian women will sing from the deepest parts of their souls? "The Barista Girl's Lament." "Sorting the Brewery's Hops." "The Hard World of an Uber Driver."

One thing is certain: Appalachian women are born singing. We have the same strong backs as our grandmaws did and put our hard times into a place where they can be dealt with, sooner or later, in ways earthy, practical, and magical.

---

12. Mike Paris, "The Dixons of South Carolina," *Old Time Music* 10 (Fall 1973): 14.

Storytelling

Across the mountains from where I live is the little town of Jonesborough, Tennessee. Jonesborough is the home of the National Storytelling Festival that happens every year in October. It features new tellers as well as the big names on the storytelling circuit. It is a guaranteed delight every year and highlights our strong oral history tradition. It isn't exclusive to here—you can check out your own town for storytelling events, if you like to be told tales. Many cities have stand-up storytelling nights for sharing spoken word performances. Tellers are some of the kindest and most generous people in the world.

Porches and kitchen tables are the first stages for storytellers. Before modern media (I'm talking about radio) and rural electrification, a visitor—whether family member from across the county line or traveling salesman-tinker—was a source of information and entertainment. The best tellers will spin a tale in the same way that wool roving is spun into yarn. A simple tale is hardly worth the telling and doesn't do much for the listener either. Characters are writ large, dangers exaggerated, and outcomes larger than life.

When I began looking at the sorts of chores that might lend themselves to singing, I came up against a pleasure I remembered from my earliest childhood, that when women gather to do work, they are more apt to talk than they are to sing. My cousin was the possessor of our great-grandmother's quilting frame, and her husband had rigged it with pulleys to move up and down over the long dining room table. Many a family story was told and repaired and retold around that old frame while little folks like me fetched the iced tea, which was always sweet, and emptied the ashtrays, which were always full. When I was old enough and skilled enough to help, the old quilting frames were only rarely used, and I was in school and only visited sometimes. These were the same stories that were told again and again on cool summer nights when the grown-ups were sitting on somebody's porch and the kids were chasing lightning bugs and running with the dog. Sometimes a voice would rise up in song and coat the darkness in something sweeter than iced tea and far older. These were not working songs, however. They were expressions of longing and regret, of love and loss, and would end softly, everyone on the porch lost in their own thoughts, their own sad histories. We are born talking, stringing our cultural pieces like beads on a thread.

Some Witchery: Finding Something That's Lost

Magic Hands for Finding will take some practice. I have always been a "finder" and am often employed to locate misplaced objects. Since my practice grows more intentional as I get older, I've devised a protocol for finding things and have given it the silly name Magic Hands.

Begin by grounding and centering, breathing deeply into your belly, and stilling yourself and your surroundings. Rub your hands together until they are pleasantly warm. Hold in your mind an image of the lost thing. Turn your hands palms-out in front of you and walk slowly through the area where the thing was last seen, if you know. Let your memory and intuition work together, especially if you are the one who lost the item. You may find your hands are tingling a bit. This technique is also useful when you can't decide what to pack for a trip or what to make for supper or which present your mother would like best.

Part 2
Skills and Work

Chapter 4

Tools, Supplies, and Techniques

This chapter begins the practical and hands-on portion of this book. We have explored some of the rich and strange cultures of the southern highlands, and now we're going to look at materials, tools, and techniques that are used to move energy around for healing, for luck, and for acquiring resources. This chapter is mostly about the tools, supplies, and techniques of my trade and how I use them. For organizational purposes I'm grouping them into the four classical elements—earth, air, fire, and water. We'll finish up with any oddments that didn't easily fit into these arbitrary boxes.

Lining the little kitchen garden at the back of the house are the broken-handled heads of once-sharp garden tools. The chicken wire fence is a graveyard of hoes, rakes, shovel heads, and pitchforks lost. None of them could be repaired in this age of planned obsolescence, or else they came to us in their brokenness, for we are odd collectors of odd things. We may have spotted one on the sidewalk or in the recycling bin at the community garden. It used to be possible to replace the handle but most tools today aren't made for that. The head can't be affixed onto the handle solidly enough to use it for hard work. Or the heads themselves are missing teeth or chunks of their forged selves.

We talk about the tools of magic, and any metaphysical shop worthy of the name will carry the modern tools of modern magic—the athames and heavy cauldrons, uncountable numbers of tarot decks, crystals, wands. Every color and size candle is available for all sorts of workings.

When we begin studying any sort of energy manipulation or magical system, it's important to start with the basics in order to create a strong foundation for our future work. There is a regional description of the dominant hand as the "strong" hand and the other hand as the "soft" hand. Years ago, I was eldered into a local Pagan community, and the person who conducted the simple ceremony asked me if I'd brought my magical tools with me. I held up my two strong hands and then touched the tips of my fingers to my forehead, my chest above my heart, and then my stomach. These are the basic tools of human beings, whether they practice magic or not. The head is vision, imagination, deep thought, and intention. The heart is the investment of emotion into the act of creation—doing the job with love and compassion. The belly is the will, the strength, the guts to bring that intention to fruition. These powerful tools work for art and parenting, for partnering and for magic. For everything, really.

Tools and Techniques of Earth

On the mountain where I grew up, there was an outcropping of rock with some trees above it. It formed a bit of shelter for the cows that were pastured there. Our neighbor called it the Knoll, and I learned its name from one of her granddaughters, who was my friend and my writing buddy. I spent a lot of summertime up there because of an unusually cool breeze and some shade. You got to this place via one of the old logging roads that crisscrossed the bald mountain. It wound past another rocky outcropping that may or may not have been an old mica mine. We were warned of it many times as we left our houses to wander the mountain—don't you dare go near that old mica mine. And we never did because we were never sure of its location, and the adults never went with us to show us because they knew we weren't to be trusted. If we had been able to locate this legendarily dangerous place, I'm sure we would have squeezed into it and had a good look around, simply because we'd been told not to. My cousin Dena and I dragged a heavy rock from near there, one we thought had cave paintings on it. Down the logging road we dragged it, dragged and rested, dragged and rested—until we got it up the bank and into my front yard. We marveled over it a good long time, but it was lost in the end, somewhere on the mountain or in the yard.

Grounding

We'll sit there together now in our mind's eye, settling ourselves under that blessed outcropping of rock as we consider the concept of earth and the tools we associate with it, both physical and metaphorical ones. Since we are sitting in this earthbound place together, let's spend a few moments looking at the importance of grounding as part of your regular practice. In so many of the classes I teach at festivals and conferences or at home, I stress the importance of this as a regular practice. This is not, strictly speaking, traditionally Appalachian. But what I learned coming up about planting your feet firmly in the dirt of home while reaching for the heavens surely prepared me for this intentional process. Also— years of being barefooted.

Imagine a warm summer morning on a smallholding in the hills. You wake and get outside as soon as you can, wearing summer clothes that consist of shorts and a sleeveless shirt, maybe some sandals or flip-flops, if your mother insisted. But these got kicked off as soon as it was practical. Dirty feet with ragged toenails—we call them toe-knives in my family—pound through all kinds of textures. Grass and gravel, mud and creek water. The horse shed has straw or dry leaves that will later be manure to avoid. We never avoided the water or mud. Each day of barefoot walking on the dirt road took us a little farther on the path from tenderfoot to the leather-footed pride of late summer when nothing could disturb our graceful stroll through the sharp-stoned edges of the gravel road.

The process of toughening our feet taught us patience as well as resilience. As my magical practice continued to develop, moving from what I'd learned in the cove by watching and listening, I needed a firm foundation to hold me up and anchor me to the ground below me—what came to be called grounding. Here is the technique I use:

I imagine tiny roots come out of the soles of my feet and wiggle their way into the sweet bosom of the earth. When they touch the ground, they get stronger and wider, and they go deep, as deep as I can imagine until I feel solid as an oak tree. I coax the energy of the earth into my feet and my legs and up into my belly. Then I breathe such big breaths of good air that my lungs are filled and my spirit settled.

Redding

Brick dust is sometimes called redding and is popular among folk magic practitioners. It is not traditional here, but it works so well as a protective element that I've adopted it for my own use. Instead of taking a hammer and busting up an old soft brick (along with my old soft fingers), you may find my technique a little easier. After a period of gentle rain, I harvest damp red clay mud. I leave it to dry until crumbly, and I grind it in a mortar with its fat pestle until the dried clay is reduced to a fine grain.

Tools

I may as well chide you now about this helpful pair of tools—a mortar and pestle. Such a handy and compact thing. If you don't have one, find yourself one. I have several, most from thrift stores. There's a small heavy one that I use for redding. A large brass one is used exclusively for poisonous plants and a recently acquired stainless steel one is handsome but too slick to be very useful. They are easily found at flea markets and thrift stores, and I suggest you get one as soon as you can.

While a sturdy grinding tool is important, a few good sharp knives are vital. These may be your everyday kitchen blades, washed thoroughly after each use and kept wickedly sharp. One for chopping, one for peeling, and a serrated one for bread because bread and butter are good for the soul and good for the belly.

These creatures of earth—steel and wood and stone—will serve you well. Take care of them as you would any tool, whether in house or garden.

Rocks and Stones

I wrote about the mythic and highly dangerous mica mine earlier in this chapter, and I want to share some of the minerals we use and used here. No fancy crystals in this folk magic, though there are many places in the region where you can pan for precious metals and stones. I work with soil, of course, and with mica, gravel, and garnets.

Mica

The beautiful big chunk of mica in my workbasket was a gift from a friend, and I have used it ever after as a reflective surface. If you don't know the virtues of mica, let me tell you about its habits, its nature. It is still used as an insulating material because it easily flakes into slivered layers, thin as glass. In fact, mica is used as windows in furnaces because it can withstand great heat. The piece I have fits nicely into my two open hands and is easily flaked with a thumbnail. That was another dire warning we received as children: don't handle mica because you might rub your eyes and the flakes would get in and you'd go blind.

In my current practice, I use mica as a reflective surface to shine light onto situations in which I need more clarity. I use it to reflect unpleasant things that may have been sent my way. Finding intact specimens the size of mine may be challenging, but it is useful regardless of size. Please be careful flaking it, though, so you don't go blind.

Garnet

Another activity of some mountain children was the finding of garnet rocks. There really are so many precious minerals here, lying on the ground, free for the taking. We'd find garnets imbedded in their matrix stone and spit on the rock to admire their color. Then we'd take them to whatever concrete block was hanging around in the yard, and one of us would go home and fetch a hammer. We'd take turns freeing those little garnets, wash them with no more than spit and pour them into a cotton bag left over from a plug of chewing tobacco. Like the cave painting stone, those little sacks of hard-won glory were left somewhere in the past.

You can see how a blood substitute stone like garnet is helpful in many situations. Garnet is also used to celebrate a girl-child's first menstrual period, something that should be honored in every possible way. It is also appropriate to celebrate the "new blood" when a child or child-in-law comes into the family through adoption or marriage. Adoption within families is a common thing in Appalachia, more so now, when addiction is ripping its way through so many mountain communities. My elder half-sister was adopted within the family, which is how I found her after our mother died.

Garnets for blood, garnets for life. A beautiful symbol as well as a magical tool.

Here in the mountains, we are suitably impressed with humility. An authentic cove doctor will speak of the Spirit flowing through them to do the work and will claim no responsibility or authority over the healing that results.

Gravel

I have written elsewhere and teach often about gravel. Gravel is everywhere, so entirely present that we rarely notice it. It lines paths and provides a nonslip surface for roads and driveways. I grew up on a dirt road that was sometimes covered in gravel by the grace of the State of North Carolina's Department of Transportation. First, a scraping machine would chug its way up one side of the horseshoe-shaped road, leveling the ruts in the roadbed. Later that day or maybe the day after, a dump truck with gravel would make several trips along the same road, leaving fresh and uneven ridges of new gravel. Cars and trucks would distribute it over the next days and everyone in the cove would complain about how rough it was on their tires. After a few rains and many bumpy trips, the gravel migrated to the edges of the road with a center ridge left mostly untouched. Occasionally, someone got a truckload of gravel for their driveway and the resulting wear-and-tear was much the same.

If you spend any time near strip-mining and mountaintop removal operations, gravel begins to take on more tragic and even sinister connotations. Gravel is the result of gouging the stone heart out of a hill and letting the rest fall away. In coal country, this activity is designed to remove the more valuable coal, and gravel is a by-product. Here in my part of Appalachia, there isn't so much coal that the mountains are ripped apart for it. Here the hills are graded and blasted and torn asunder for the parking lot, the road-bed, or your driveway. There's a highway here, down almost into the foothills, that winds its way into the high country from Interstate 40. You can see steel-caged stone there waiting to be bought and sold, moved to build a wall or house. They are waiting for a truck heavy enough to haul them away. The quarry is usually right behind the sales area, stripped of vegetation and soil, its crumbling center strange in the light of day.

Gravel is the bones of the hills, broken for our enrichment. Gravel is the heart of the mountain, the broken heart of home. This makes it all less humble and more ominous. It is certainly a non-renewable resource and one whose removal spoils and destroys the resources around it. Old hills, once as high as the Alps, laid low for their innards. Laid low forever, never to be rebuilt.

The more I think on gravel, the more I honor both what it is and what it does. It feels more potent than diamonds and just as bloody—though the lifeblood of the ecosystem is always green in my mind's eye. Gravel is sometimes called crushed stone, but these are two somewhat different things. Gravel is naturally occurring and is dug up and pulled out. But there is a finite amount of it and humans need more and more of it. The result of those market-driven forces is the product called crushed stone, which is exactly what it sounds like. Larger mined stone is crushed with heavy machinery to become gravel That difference is interesting but I'm not sure if it feels important enough when using gravel for the purposes we're exploring. You think about it and decide for yourself. Is there a significant energetic feel to the two things? Is it enough different to spend time sourcing broken rock? If so, do so.

If gravel is the bone and heart of the hills that I call home, I feel an obligation to use these materials carefully, intentionally. These ragged bits of stone are heavy in my hand and not exactly picturesque. I lick them, as I did half a century or more ago. The spit changes the color temporarily and I feel the grit on my tongue. I swallow hard and think about the taste of the soil and how precious that stuff is here and everywhere.

Bones and heart. I think of strength and of character. Of integrity. I'd use this dear old stone when I was lacking in those attributes or if someone I cared for needed that support from me.

When friends or clients have big decisions to make, I will sometimes suggest that they gather a small pile of gravel and place it around a lovely bowl, somewhere on their kitchen table or their desk. When they consider the list of possibilities, something that feels right in their gut requires a piece of gravel placed in the bowl. When the bowl is full of gravel bits, they are ready to make a considered decision because they have given their soul time to parse the next step in their personal journey. This simple stone can hold all our dreams, as well as our sorrows when we remember its beginnings as the heart of an ancient mountain.

River Rock

Part of my family spent a good deal of each summer at a local campground, enjoying the peace and quiet, drinking a lot of beer and liquor. What I chiefly remember about those summer days were the rocks that lined the banks of the little river for which the campground was named. They were smooth and mostly round, soft even in their heaviness. We always went home with dozens of the best ones, and used them to line flower gardens. I still love and collect them and use them still for their beauty and for their memory of the water that changed them, slowly, inevitably. They feature in cairn building too when I honor the best autumn tree in the neighborhood or mark the final resting place of a beloved pet.

River rock. Gravel. Garnets. Mica. The stone of the land that owns me, that holds the bones and ashes of my forebears. How could we not use these fragments of our holy land to do our holy work?

Tools and Techniques of Air

I start out so many classes by helping the attendees relax and focus by teaching them a technique called Four-Square Breathing. I talk them through it first. Inhale for a count of four. Hold for a count of four. Exhale for a count of four. And rest for a count of four. Ready? Inhale two three four. And hold two three four. Exhale two three four. And rest two three four. Now breathe deeply and normally.

It is always interesting to watch their faces as we repeat the process, which I usually do three times. Consternation, confusion, exasperation. Then the softening as they realize it isn't a hard or complicated process. That softening helps them focus and be present for whatever I am teaching.

Breathing

Breath is an integral part of traditional Appalachian healing. According to Appalachian folklore, one of the gifts of someone who is the seventh son of a seventh son or the seventh daughter of a seventh daughter is the ability to use their breath to cure diseases, one of them being thrush, sometimes called thrash. Thrush is a fungal infection, one of the dreaded candidas (like yeast infections), and was a constant threat in rural areas. It is easily cleared up now, and generally the symptoms are more annoying than threatening. But for a suckling infant years ago, the fungus might inhibit breast or bottle feeding because it is sometimes painful. An infant who can't feed is in a risky situation. The child with the special gift would be brought in to blow in the baby's mouth and thereby cure the thrash. I've talked to several adults who were hauled around as children to cure the thrash. It seems to have worked often enough that people kept up the practice.

It makes sense that breath and breathing are associated with healing in southern Appalachian communities that base so much on the Bible. We recall how humans were created, according to the Genesis story that is itself problematic in so many ways. The Bible reads, "And the LORD God formed man from the dust of the ground, and breathed into his nostrils the breath of life; and man became a living soul."[13]

Blood and breath figure prominently in so many aspects of folk healing globally and ours is no exception. Inspiration is, quite literally, "breathing in." And expiration is breathing out as well as removing life from your credit card or elderly milk in the refrigerator. It

---

13. Genesis 2:7 (King James Version).

bears with it not only the gift of life but a life ensouled, as Genesis so aptly illustrates.

The woods are said to breathe, as does a good stand of corn, and there is a sense that it isn't only humans who perceive that precious action but that the trees and corn and everything living around us is breathing in and out, living and sacred. Ensouled, as we humans are. We know trees exhale the gases we need and we exhale the ones for them, which is why we call the Amazon Basin the "lungs of the world." It's this exchange of holy breath that keeps us upright, with our ragged souls somehow still attached. As a woman who has lived her life under sweet gum and poplars, holly and old apple trees, I am here to testify that I ken this on the innermost level of myself. In. Out. Holy, holy, holy.

Feathers

My research as a spellcatcher takes me back to the home countries every few years. I talk to folks in pubs and folk museums and at farms and allotments. At Anne Hathaway's farm outside Stratford-upon-Avon, we had to be very careful as there was a ferocious outbreak of hoof-and-mouth disease. The front garden was beautifully arranged, as most English gardens are. Over in the vegetable section—a kitchen garden as lovely as the day—there was a curious contraption. It was a medium-sized potato that had a length of narrow rope pulled through the center, the ends of which were tied off to the fence. It hung suspended there and large-ish feathers had been stuck in it so that it turned in the breeze. Can you picture it? Chicken tail feathers, duck and goose feathers, a few from ravens or swans, spinning in the cool air of the English countryside like a bird from outer space. I had to know what it was and gardeners and farmers are some of my favorite people to talk to, so I went in search of someone on the grounds. Turns out it is a medieval bird-scarer and was cheap, easy to replace, and simple to create.

The following is obviously not a traditional Appalachian folk-way, at least as far as I know. No one has ever told me that they or their family did it or that they had heard of it before. I use a similar feathered critter to send a job of work out into the world and to keep the spell energized and activated. It spins in my garden as long as the potato and the feathers last. Sometimes I write an intention directly onto the potato and sometimes I write it on a slip of paper and jam it in the rope hole. That extraordinary bird-scarer was too dynamic not to repurpose it as a magical tool. And it really does keep the birds away, except from the elderberries. They are irresistible.

Tasting Wind

Old-timers set great store by tasting the wind, feeling it brought them knowledge about weather, bird and animal migrations, and even prophetic information about the future of their land or their family. It was a way to commune with God and self and nature. Tasting the wind is an old art that is not much practiced these days. I have set myself the goal of practicing this folkway enough in the next few years so that I can pass it on. It requires a good sense of smell and the patience to connect a particular smell—of snow or rain or soon-lightning—to the subsequent event. You stand in as clear a place as possible, where the breeze can easily find your nose. Breathe deeply through your nostrils. Exhale. Breathe next time through your barely opened mouth. Exhale. Alternate these techniques until you catch a whiff or taste of something on the wind. Then observe and remember.

Tools and Techniques of Fire

I grew up on the side of a mountain, a mountain mostly covered with trees. Outside the kitchen door, there was a slice of undeveloped woodland between our house and the next one over. Our own property was also wooded, as was the property on the other side that held a ramshackle wooden farmhouse built in the earliest days of the cove's habitation. Our house too was made of wood. Wood and woods. A blessing when we needed sticks or shade or the dried leaves for pony bedding. We walked beyond our own property most years to find and cut down a Christmas tree. In the autumn, when thousands of people still descend on the southern highlands to view the colors of the leaves as they die, the forests around us were also a source of apprehension because of the tinder their summer lives had produced. It is still called fire season hereabouts, and there were no hydrants or fire departments within call of the cove folk. Most wildfires were fought by volunteers and most fires were caused by carelessness—a campfire left smoldering, a landowner burning off a field or pile of trash while enjoying "a cold one" or two or three.

Fire is hard to control because it is unpredictable. Of the four elements I'm using here, it is the one most likely to get out of hand. It is warming in the fireplace, but have a care about creosote buildup in your chimney. Falling asleep to the smell of wood smoke and a faint orange glow in the window was never easy. I can't remember if we were told to do this by our ne'er-do-well parents, but I would put my most precious things in a box under my bed, easily accessible if we had to clamber down the bank to the old station wagon and leave the cove—and our house—behind. One year the treasures included a sixty-four-count box of real Crayola crayons, new ones I had bought with my own money at the drugstore near my cousin's house. I wasn't evacuating without those beauties

We had damaging wildfires here in 2016. More than sixteen thousand acres burned. The worst happened after the bulk of the fires were under control. Sweet old Gatlinburg was set afire by careless kids on the mountain at Chimney Tops. Thousands of buildings were damaged or destroyed outright and fourteen people died. Fire on the mountain is always something to take seriously.

We often talk of fire symbolically, equating it with passion and vivacity. Wildfire is an unknown, less to be dreaded than to prepare for if you live in a fire-prone area. Fire is a powerful tool and, like all tools, must be used with consideration. When we ponder both its power and its symbolic importance, we learn to embrace our own fiery spirits to the aid of healing and magic. We can write our intentions and prayers on slips of paper and burn those bits to remove that which no longer serves us and holds back our progress. We can send our prayers to the spirit world through the cleansing power of fire.

Candles

Dressing candles with special oils enhances the ability of fire and light to effect change and healing. I am especially fond of three herbal oils for candle dressing: vervain, rue, and mugwort. I make those oils by harvesting the fresh herb and stuffing a canning jar three-quarters full with it. I add inexpensive vegetable oil to fill the jar up, leaving a little space, called headroom, at the top. The lid is screwed on securely and it is given some good shakes. The jar is placed somewhere away from direct sunlight. It is shaken every couple of days and will be left on the plant material for a moon cycle. If you lay it down on a new moon, it will be ready and at full potency on the following new moon.

Other people may have a different duration, but a moon cycle is what I was taught and it is easy to remember. It is also wise to label your jars, even if you think you'll remember. Once you've shaken a jar of plant material in oil for a month, it's often hard to tell what the original plant was. A little strip of masking tape and a black pen will do the trick. After a month, pour the oil off the plant material into a clean jar. Pour it through a strainer to get rid of the last bit of plant material because that goo may mold. That doesn't really matter since you're not ingesting the finished product, but it is unsightly and can make your oil smell "off." You may choose to refrigerate your oils, but I've found that storing them in a cool, dark place is usually sufficient. You can read about my favorite herbal oils in chapter 6.

You can use any size candle for candle magic. Use a birthday candle in an aluminum cupcake holder for something quick and easy. Tealights have a soft glow, are easily dressed with a dab of oil, and burn out in about an hour. Seven-day candles are harder to dress but they burn for far longer. With a bit of luck and some wiggling, you may be able to slide the whole wax cylinder out of the jar by its wick, dress it, and slide it back in. If you make your own candles, you can add any oil to the wax before you pour. This can sometimes result in the glass cracking as the candle burns, so make sure to put a plate underneath and place the whole shebang on a fireproof surface. Fat white emergency candles are readily available, inexpensive, and easy to dress and will burn for several hours.

Never leave a burning candle unattended, not even a seven-day candle in a stout glass jar. If a job of work requires a long burn, I will stay with it and place it in the kitchen sink, in case I somehow forget about it. I am aware that many people light a seven-day candle, put it on a protective dish and let it burn. I do not because I have seen too many of them shatter and because of my childhood experiences.

The Energy Trap

Tealights, whether wax or battery-operated, are handy things, and I use them in one of my favorite workings: the Energy Trap. I've assembled these in many places or taught someone to do it for themselves. It was conjured up for a client who felt her house was full of negative energy. In this case, the energy was stale and bunged up and needing a good stirring up and clearing out. (I later discovered that her husband was also embezzling money from his workplace. That couldn't have been helping the home situation much either.)

I've been using it since that first experiment, and it has proved to be very effective. It acts as a filter for stagnant energy in your home, energy that can be misconstrued as spirit activity. Here are directions for constructing and using one. You'll need a flat, round reflective surface (the bottom of a throw-away pie pan is the best, but you can use a round mirror too), three flat black rocks, a tealight candle (my preference is a battery-operated one because they are safe around children and animals), and two grades of salt (inexpensive table salt and ice cream salt, for instance). Place the reflective surface on a flat surface—put it on a high shelf out of sight, if that's needed, or put it in a prominent place to add the energy of your thoughts every time you see it. Put the three flat stones in the center of the mirror. Pour the heavy salt in a circle around the stones. Pour the table salt on the outer edge of the mirror. Now, place the tealight on top of the stones in the center and light it or turn it on. The theory behind this trap is that stagnant and unhealthy energy is drawn to the light, filtered first through the stones, then filtered through the rough salt, filtered a final time through the fine salt. It is then reflected back out into the area as clean, useable energy. You can keep one of these going all the time, but it isn't necessary. You'll feel the difference in a few days. If you are moving into a new place or if your office environment is harsh, run the trap for at least a moon cycle. If you run it longer than that, change the salt every moon cycle.

Sacred Smoke

A section on fire isn't complete without a brief paragraph on sacred smoke. As we continue to refrain from using white sage as a smudge or palo santo as an incense (for cultural as well as environmental reasons), it is good to remember that sacred smoke is used by many cultures for ritual purification and each culture uses materials that are native to them for this purpose.

I make my Appalachian version by combining equal parts mountain mint (*Pycnanthemum virginianum*), mugwort (*Artemisia vulgaris*), and rabbit tobacco (*Pseudognaphalium obtusifolium*), all dried. I burn it on a charcoal disk or throw it on the fire in a burning bowl or sturdy cauldron. The smell of mountain sanctity, sure enough.

The Tools and Techniques of Water

Let's go back to the cove for this last section. Our house was situated at the head of the cove and we had a city water line instead of a spring or well. Because we were higher up the hill, our water pressure was only really strong at night. We didn't have a bathroom, so the water use was concentrated in cooking and washing dishes and clothes. We bathed in a pan of water in the kitchen sink, and I washed my long hair in the sink too. The water lines weren't buried deeply enough for a cold winter with prolonged freezes, which meant the water line was sometimes solid in the worst weather. When that happened we would take plastic milk jugs and the big spaghetti pot to the most magical place on the mountain: the springhouse near my cousin's trailer.

I don't know who built the stone springhouse but it was regularly tended, whitewashed, repaired. I remember it as a small stone house about four feet wide and three feet high. There was a wooden door with a door-screen, and it swung from one side in the middle of the rock face of the spring. The door was secured with a piece of skinny wood that was turned up to open the door and turned sideways to latch the door after you'd dipped your water. A ledge ran along the edge of the springhead, inside the little house. Sometimes there was a cup in there, so you could get a drink of water. Sometimes there was a snake there, staying cool on a hot summer day. The springhouse was set into the side of a low hill and it was shaded by the trees above and around it.

You approached the spring by a footpath through a mostly unused pasture. It seems like I always knew about the spring, but someone must've told me about it at some point. Unlike the dangerous mica, we were never warned about the dangers of the spring, only told to be very careful about closing the door. That springhouse was helpful and somehow safe, which kept it magical and full of delicious promise. Years later when I learned about well dressing and the folkloric importance placed on those portals where water rises up through the earth to reveal itself, I thought of the care blandished on that little springhouse by the unknowable adults who tended it. Is it any wonder these liminal places are tended and decorated and believed to contain powerful spirits?

As I ponder the importance of water to Appalachian folkways, I begin to suspect that this held the key to Scots-Irish and Cherokee (and other Native Americans) interactions. The idea of "going to water" to pray for and achieve healing is a strong one in Cherokee culture. Marry that to the British veneration of water sources and we begin to see how the streams flow together to impact folk healing and folk magic in the region. Love, healing, transformation—notions that still affect the southern highlands today.

In 2014, there was a massive chemical spill on the Elk River in West Virginia. The Elk is a tributary of the Kanawha, the river that provides water to the state capitol in Charleston. The spill affected more than three hundred thousand people. The people got one lucky break in that the chemical had a strong licorice smell, even in tiny amounts, so—unlike many of the contaminants in the nation's waterways—this one was noticeable. The chemical in question was used to separate coal from rock fragments and had been deemed to be harmless. Except it wasn't and it had never been thoroughly tested. Three hundred thousand people.[14] A sterling example that not everyone in Appalachia cares about water.

In addition to the common ways in which humans use water, we have adapted some different water-based materials for a number of uses. We'll take a look at those now.

Dishwater

This water was the greasy, globby, lukewarm stuff left in your washpan and is less available than it once was, in this time of dish-washing appliances, but it is still easily acquired. Dishwater

---

14. Ned Resnikoff, "West Virginia chemical spill leaves 300,000 without clean water," MSNBC, January 30, 2014, http://www.msnbc.com/all/west-virginia-chemical-spill-water.

is like good compost and contains all the building blocks of strong magic and healing. With an accompanying dishrag, much can be accomplished. A rag soaked in dishwater is slapped against a tree trunk or flat rock to call rain. Rubbing warts with a dishrag sopping wet with dishwater and then burying the rag somewhere off your land will take away the wart. I have never known this to work, but it is a popular technique here in the hills. Try it for yourself and see if it works for you because many people swear by it.

Dishwater is the compound (water and soap) that is used to remove food bits from dishes and cookware, to clean them in readiness for the next meal. If we use that as a baseline, we can consider using it to remove what we need removed from our lives and to clean up messes. With or without a handy rag, use dishwater with these intentions and you can use any opportunity to clean the kitchen not as a chore but as a chance to energetically tidy up your life. Before you dump that gray water down the drain, put the fingertips of your strong hand in the water and move them in a counterclockwise circle, all the while thinking of your intention. When you pour the water from the pan, say goodbye to whatever you are dumping from your life, rinse your hands, put on a little lotion, and move on.

Clean water flowing into your sink is a gift not everyone receives. Take a tip from the sweet well-dressing customs in Britain and hang a loop of fresh greens from your garden or even silk flowers around the spigot to remind yourself of the blessing that is fresh water. And, for heaven's sake, don't waste water by leaving it running when you're not actively using it. Water is precious as well as sacred. We'd all be wise to sharply consider our use of water.

Willow Water

The willow tree is one of the brightest things in the spring landscape, sporting eye-catching green cascades of new leaves. It is a
plant that grows by the water, trailing its long loose branches into
available water. It's the bark that most interests us. It contains sal-
icin, a chemical compound like the active ingredient in aspirin,
salicylic acid. It has been used medicinally for centuries, but we're
concerning ourselves with its uses in Appalachian folklore. Prepare willow water in the spring of the year, when the leaves are
that perfect bright green. Snip off the ends of a good handful of
those flowing branches and fill a canning jar about three-quarters
full. Fill it the rest of the way with fresh spring or well water and
leave it in a cool place for seven days. This water can be refriger-
ated at any time and is used to soothe and calm. Soak a soft cotton
cloth in this water and lie down with it on your forehead as you
rest. Soak your busy feet in a pan of it, leaving the green leaves in as
a tonic for your eyes. Bathe your wrists and the inside bend of your
elbows to ease yourself after a day of difficult or stressful work.

Ditchwater, Stump Water, Stormwater

Three other waters are popular in our folklore: ditchwater, stump
water, and stormwater (including snow). They are sovereign elixirs
that I hope you will try.

Ditchwater is the stuff that is found in the wet, early spring
and is full of life. Frog eggs, insects, algae, all the stuff of new and
vibrant life. Don't ingest it—instead use it to inspire your creative
self, to keep a new project juicy. Fill a canning jar with some and
put it on your desk or work space. Replace it every few days to
keep it lively and wholesome.

Stump water is the rainwater that collects in the basin of an old stump. Rainwater that doesn't touch the soil is thought to be cleaner than some other water. Stumps are not common for many of us, which makes this water more valuable in its rarity. Stump water is primarily used as a folk remedy for various skin disorders. Freckles were not popular with young ladies who wanted unblemished skin. Teenagers prone to breakouts of pimples, blackheads, and the like used stump water for cleaning their faces of these blemishes. It has been used for poison ivy and for insect bites, though there are herbal remedies that work better for both of those conditions. Stump water was also believed to remove warts. With so many wart remedies, it seems there was a near-constant concern about the result of that virus. Stump water from different trees may have different properties: oak stump for wisdom and strength, willow stump for flexibility and connection across realms, and maple stump water for sweetening the bitter parts of life.

Water collected during a rainstorm and melted snow gathered from a snowfall contain the power of these meteorological events. The rainwater is gathered during the storm, adding an extra ingredient—courage—to the movement and energy of the storm. Snow water must be collected in a clean bowl as the snow falls and not simply scooped up from the yard after the snow has stopped falling. Both waters are used for healing various ailments because they arrive from the heavens (or heaven) in glory and authority.

Other Helpful and Traditional Waters

Forge Water

If you know a blacksmith, you are blessed, my friend. Bring that person offerings of what he or she likes and spend some time watching this old and important work. It is powerfully elemental, making hot fire with wood and air, using that fire to purify and form iron, which is cooled with water. You may ask for a small jar of that water and use it in the same way—as a placeholder for the elemental powers of creation and to strengthen your will. Dress candles with it. Dab it on your pulse points and temples. Remind yourself of the forces that both are and move the universe—and that you are part of all that.

Mill Water

Mill water is working water from a mill race. It moves the great wheel that grinds the grain or generates electricity. It can be used in many ways. Try it to aid in completing monotonous tasks or sticking with long-range goals, or let it inspire you as you move your own wheel to generate movement in your life.

Morning Dew

Morning dew holds a fine place in the world's folklore. From the time I was a child, I was advised to always wash my face in the dew on the first of May. I would pat my hands on the damp grass, palms down, and then rub the dew onto my cheeks. I still do this every year and taught my daughter to do the same. This annual dampening was supposed to guarantee a beautiful face and thereby a beautiful life. I'm sure it works every single time.

The Land beneath the Waters

There is sometimes an uneasy interaction between water and soil, and that should be mentioned here. Many of the lakes in the region are human-made, the larger ones are mostly the product of the Tennessee Valley Authority's efforts at rural electrification in the 1940s. Roosevelt signed the New Deal plan into law. Smaller lakes were constructed for many reasons, including recreation and livestock watering. All these created lakes and ponds have something in common: the drowning of good land, making it incapable of behaving as land does, and there is sometimes a sense of the land's resentment there.

Near me there is a popular lake that we frequented in my high school years, though now it is part of a gated community and no longer accessible to the likes of us. Before the Enka corporation bought the land for homes for their white-collar employees and made the lake a focal point for what was then called Enka Village, part of that place was a dairy farm owned by a cousin of mine named Belle Ballard. She sold the property and moved the farm some miles away. As with many of these flooding events, the buildings were left standing, which always feels a little creepy after the fact. We like to imagine an intact ghostly farm waiting there under the calm surface of the lake, not considering what decades of being under water will do to wooden structures. It is there, waiting, lonely. Fanciful but oddly compelling. Whether the sense of resentment is a longing for old times or a genuine feel for and connection to the lost land beneath the waters may be a matter for myth and legend. But many people speak of it and are sincere in their belief. It also makes for some sweet tunes and ghostly tales.

Some Witchery: Attracting and Manifesting

Attraction magic is an important thing to master. There are all sorts of things you'll want to bring into your life as you live it, whether it's a new place to live or to work or friends to share your good times and comfort you in the hard ones. Appalachian folk magic has some interesting love spells and getting your partner back spells and what I think of as "Jolene spells"—magic to keep your romantic partner from straying. You can find those in lots of places but I do not recommend their use. When you tie your energy into luring in a particular person that you've set your hat for (though that person has no interest in you), you are asking for trouble. And if your partner is swayed by Ms. Jolene's seductive ways, your magical attention will be better used to focus on the other resources you need to live a full and beautiful life. So the following attracting spell is not about that. It is about attracting the resources I just mentioned: job or better job, new or first house, or other things you are choosing to manifest or attract.

Pie Plates and Candles

I do a lot of work with reflective surfaces—mirrors, aluminum pie pans, and the like. Take one of those and add to it some dressed candles. I'd use green for a job, yellow for a cheery new place to live. I'd do a combination of styles of candles, depending on what was available: anything from a battery tealight to a big pillar candle will do the trick. Dress them with a strong oil. My favorite is rue or woad oil, but I might consider mugwort oil if part of the manifestation involves keeping a dream alive and vital. Sprinkle the working surface with usnea or moss so that the thing you're calling to you "sticks" with you. I might even add some cockleburs for extra sticking. As always, don't leave the candles alone. Sit with them and set your intention as they burn, running it through your head as you watch the flames. Review the specifics of what you need—a range of salaries or specific working hours for a new job, location and price range for different housing, and so on.

The Open-Mouthed Purse

You'll need to gather up a little coin purse (the best are those old-fashioned ones with a little clasp on top) that can open into a wide "mouth," shiny coins of any denomination (even chocolate ones will work), a small mirror, and shiny bits (Mardi Gras beads, for example).

I keep one of these going all the time—it's easy. Put it anywhere that you will see it and add your energy to it. Set the little purse upright on the mirror with its mouth open. Drop some shiny coins in its mouth and set all manner of shiny things, like those golden Mardi Gras beads, around it. Keep a lookout for shiny coins coming to you as change and add them to the purse. Any "found" coins also go in and around the purse. Be sure to welcome all your abundance, prosperity, and money energy.

Chapter 5

Mountain Kitchen Witchery

There are many valuable skills that have been passed down through the generations, and there are some that are mostly lost or only lightly practiced now. We will look at food ways, family traditions, and witchery, as centered in the kitchen. Let's begin with food because it is almost suppertime and I'm getting a little hungry.

We eat good here, as we say. Though we have a justifiable reputation for pockets of rural poverty and hunger, the cooking here is simple but filling.

I'm often accused of code-switching: moving from native dialect and word usage to a more conventional speech that is more easily understood by people outside the area and less likely to be mocked. This means I sometimes translate what is said to me. An example is the naming of daily meals. *Breakfast* is the same word in either usage, but we call the meal in the middle of the day *dinner* and the one at the end of the day *supper*. If a friend invites me to dinner, I will first express my delight and gratitude and then ask what time I should arrive and what I should bring. This solves the problem of which meal they mean—the noontime one or the

evening one. I am open to invitations to either or both, in case you
need to know that.

We will look at the sorts of foods and their preparation that are
popular among rural people and working-class urban people (the
folks who left the farms and moved into town to work in the mills,
for instance). There is not enough room here to do a thorough job,
so I have listed some excellent books in the recommended reading
section by folks who know their stuff. I will offer you some of the
practices I do or have done, as well as the ones with the best stories.

Foodstuffs

My father did not cook, which was a shame because my mother
was a dreadful cook. He did have three dishes that he made, and
two of them featured cabbage. He sliced potatoes and chopped
cabbage and then threw the lot into a cast-iron skillet that had a
little water boiling in it. Then he turned down the heat, added salt
and pepper and a chunk of butter, and waited. He called it stewed
potatoes and it was always filling and delicious. On lucky days, he'd
throw in a little fried fatback pork.

His other signature dishes were creamed corn and coleslaw,
or (as we called it) cold slaw. Fresh corn—preferably white horse
corn, a silage variety that also makes a fine cornmeal—was scraped
across a special tool called a corn cutter that separated the kernels
from the cob. The kernels were thrown into a hot pan with some
butter, salt, pepper, a little flour, and milk. It was stewed until the
corn was tender and there was a light gravy.

The only other thing I remember him making was a special coleslaw that was grated cabbage, a chopped-up apple, and mayonnaise.

My family has a tasty and effective cold remedy. You will need
a couple of medium-size Irish (white) potatoes, a strong onion,

some fresh garlic, a couple of eggs, salt, and pepper. Slice the onion thinly and cook it slowly in a warm pan, in a little fat. Use the stinkiest onion you can find. When the onion starts to look transparent, add in the thickly sliced potato and the garlic. Cook at medium heat until the potatoes are mostly cooked but still very firm in the center. Add in the eggs and stir the whole mess together. Pour it onto a dish and add lots of black pepper and some salt. Eat it as hot as you can. My family swears by this as a cold remedy, and I've used it many times to open up my sinuses, clear congestion, and get me on the road to wellness. It has the advantage of being easy to cook and tasty to eat, even if you don't have a cold.

Cabbage was and is an important ingredient in the southern highlands. In addition to my daddy's fancy cooking, we had neighbors who regularly made kraut in big stoneware crocks and canned a relish called piccalilli and another called chow-chow. I have our neighbor Mrs. Hilton's chow-chow recipe, a gift from her granddaughter. The relish was spooned on top of soup beans mostly, giving the well-seasoned and well-cooked dried beans a pleasant, tangy crunch.

Beans are so important in the region that it is impossible to overstate how much and how often we ate them. Soup beans are made with dried beans, the seeds that grow in the green bean pods that are familiar to most of us. They keep almost indefinitely and are cheap and easy to prepare. The cleaned beans are placed in a large pot of water and are left simmering on the cookstove until they are tender and a rich broth has formed. They are traditionally seasoned with pork fat and black pepper. They are full of fiber and nutritious. They are often served with a cake of corn bread, which we will discuss in a moment.

Another way of keeping beans over a long winter was to string perfect green beans and hang them up to dry, pod and all. A mountain kitchen would often have a curtain of these bean strings, ready to be washed and thrown into a pot of boiling water to cook until tender. They are called leather britches, and there is a trick to drying and cooking them. They must have exactly the right amount of time drying to preserve them but not dry them out entirely. There must still be a little vitality in the pods so that they are leathery but not crumbly. Cooking them in a pot with strong seasonings is best. Be generous with both fat and salt. And chop up some fresh onion on them when they're served up. Dry them out of the sun and pack them away in a canning jar or brown paper bag to store them. They have a different taste and texture than fresh beans. All beans are a good source of protein and are a cheap way to feed a large family that preserved and ate every bit of food that they grew or foraged.

Corn bread is a gift from heaven and you can take that to the bank. There are two schools of thought about corn bread and never the twain shall meet: some people put sugar or honey in the batter, and some do not. Corn bread—with or without the addition of a sweetener—is best cooked in a preheated cast-iron frying pan in a fast oven. I put the pan on the eye of the stove and heat up enough fat (lard is best, but vegetable shortening will do) for the batter and to coat the pan thoroughly. While that is melting, I mix the batter. Mine has cornmeal, a little flour, an egg or two, and buttermilk. I add cracklings on New Year's Day but rarely at other times. I stir the batter by hand and pour on half the melted fat from the frying pan. I pour the batter into the hot pan and slide it into a hot oven. It bakes until the center comes out clean when tested and the crust is crisp and sizzling. The cake, or pone, is turned out on a plate and served immediately, hot as the devil's big toe. If there is any left over, it can be reheated and served with butter and something sweet, like honey. My father liked it crumbled into a glass with sweet milk on it, for breakfast or dessert.

Corn bread and biscuits are a source of pride for many mountain cooks. Praise them lavishly if these breads are offered to you and you'll be sure to get them again.

Canning

Some foods were dried, many meats were smoked in a smokehouse, and many others were canned. There are several good books on these processes in the recommended reading section. I'll write from my personal experience and leave you to experiment further, if you so choose.

Canning is enjoying a resurgence in popularity these days and I am grateful for that. There are several methods for processing canned food and we'll review a couple of them here. The water bath method requires no special equipment and consists of placing your freshly canned food products into a hot water bath—a big pot of boiling water—and boiling the water to sterilize the contents. This simple method is appropriate for jams, jellies, and other high sugar content foods. Most everything else will benefit from being canned under pressure, in a special pot called a pressure canner. These are heavy and have a lid that snaps shut, sealing the boiling water into the pot to sterilize your jars of food. The agricultural extension office (sometimes called the cooperative extension) in your community is your friend, and you should have the pressure gauge on your canner checked by them every year.

Mason jars are everywhere these days. There are chain restaurants that use them to serve drinks and collectors who go crazy about the vintage and antique ones. They are more properly called canning jars, Mason being a brand name. I was given a fanciful canning jar chalice that is a Mason jar on a glass stem, like a wineglass.

They are handy for more than canning, of course, and are regularly used for storing all sorts of things, from dried beans to buttons. They are sturdy and don't break easily, even if they are dropped. You can put refrigerator jelly in them and freeze them. They are versatile and relatively inexpensive, especially if you get them at thrift stores and flea markets. The screw-on top consists of two pieces: the lid and the ring. These are usually available at hardware and grocery stores.

Cast-Iron Stoves and Cookware

My cousin Bosie had a wood cookstove on her side porch. Her primary stove, the one in the kitchen, was electric, which was quick and easy to use. But that old wood cookstove held a place of honor and she would fire it up, usually in the winter and it was always a pleasure to step into her old log house and enjoy the memories that drifted through your head at the smell of that particular combination of wood smoke and pork fat. Her son and his family moved into the house after she died. I wonder if they ever cook on that stove on the porch or if it is even there.

Another neighbor cooked exclusively on a small wood cookstove, and there was always a stack of kindling outside her front door. I sometimes helped her bake cakes in that oven, as well as bread, biscuits, and corn bread. It was always delicious and I was fascinated with her skill in judging the oven's temperature. She would put in the kindling, light a fire in it using those stout wooden matches and continue feeding in the kindling, along with larger pieces of wood, through the little doorway of the firebox until the temperature felt right for whatever she was baking. She would open the oven door when experience told her it was likely to be the right temperature. She used the ends of her apron to open the heavy oven door then put her bare hand inside for a moment. This way she determined if it was a fast (hot) oven or a slow (cooler) one.

Different things cook at different temperatures and years of experience made her adept with that little stove. It stayed warm most of the time and there was usually a pot of water on the back, ready to wash dishes or a child's dirty hands and face.

No review of Appalachian cooking, however cursory, is complete without at least a mention of cast-iron cookware. Heavy as sin, durable, magnificent, a cast-iron frying pan, perfectly seasoned, is a thing of beauty and a joy forever. Even heat distribution as well as an ability to hold heat makes it a good choice for cooks at any level of experience. We are talking about bare cast-iron, not enameled ware. The key to using cast iron is the layer of acquired seasoning of the utensil and that is why they are never washed in soapy water and never ever put into a dishwasher. Ever. Hot water and plain steel wool on the stuck spots is all that's needed. My cousin Bosie was visited one day by a traveling pot-and-pan salesman. He scoffed at her cast-iron dutch oven and proclaimed that there was enough built-up food in the pan that he could make a pot of soup by simply boiling water.

Cast-iron cookware is passed down through families, with a daughter sometimes getting the heavier pieces as her mother's arms get too soft to pick them up. Prized and tended, cast-iron pans are one of the treasures of Appalachian food culture.

And don't forget—don't try to help out by putting your sweetie's pan in the dishwasher to get rid of that greasy coating. Because your sweetie will kill you.

Some projects were too big for a kitchen and were undertaken outside over a fire. Apple butter and sorghum take a long time to process and both act like napalm if you get too close and they splash onto your bare skin. Both are cooked in mighty cauldrons—the same ones that were used on laundry day—over open fires, outside, then bottled up for sale or use. If you ever have the opportunity to watch them being made or to help with that process, you will be astounded with the amount of work and attention they take and how delicious the finished product is.

Stepping Out of the Kitchen: Birth and Death

Ceremonies and superstitions around the beginning and end of life loom large in the folkways of the southern highlands. The yarb women that we speak of so often were and are women who tend a community, filling many important roles in the life of a holler or a township. Sometimes a group of women came together for a particular task. Sometimes a woman worked solo or was accompanied by an informal apprentice, often a child or grandchild, who shadowed her to learn her ways.

I recommend the book *A Midwife's Tale: The Life of Martha Ballard, Based on Her Diary, 1785–1812* by Laurel Thatcher Ulrich. It is a heart-rending account of birth, death, and everything in between. So much of our study of history is concerned with war and colonization that accounts of the work and lives of hardworking women are often lost. But that work is the bedrock of any culture and should be celebrated and the practitioners honored—and remembered.

In the United States, we are coming to terms with our fear and trepidation around end-of-life issues, including death. You can take training now in death midwifery, and there are resources on green burials, at-home care, and the like. I always maintain that in the South, especially here in the mountains, we understand what to do with death. When someone dies here, we are not frozen into inaction, confused by what should or could be done.

We cook.

Then we bring that food, along with some sort of drink, to the house of the deceased, where the family will have gathered.

This seems odd to some people outside of the region whose own culture suggests that the recently bereaved require privacy, instead of making fresh deviled eggs or your mama's special spice cake. We gather up what we need and head to the house. There is always someone there and we are greeted with handshakes, hugs, tears. We make our way into the kitchen and find a place in the already-full refrigerator for anything we've brought that requires that. As we do that, we are told to "eat something" or "fill you up a plate now." You are expected to drink something too—there will be big Solo cups and a cooler full of ice. Iced tea will always be present. In my part of the mountains, iced tea is always sweet tea, but a quest for better general health has introduced "unsweet" iced tea to our Southern palates. You can tell much about the family if the offerings are various soft drinks (we tend to call all sodas Cokes) but no alcohol.

You then take your food with you as you make your way to the center of the action, to where everyone is gathered. You'll speak to relatives and family friends. You will finally arrive at the knee of the person in the family who holds the story of the death. You will hug that person and try your best not to drop potato salad from your plate. You will murmur condolences and apologies. And then you will find a place to sit and you will eat your food and listen, quietly and intently. You may interject and nod but your role here is to witness. In this sad land of mist and removals, to stand as witness is sometimes all we can do. Appalachia is a mythic place, a soiled and desperate outpost where the American dream goes to die and to be reborn. Recent arrivals will swear they know the ins and outs of the hills after a few years of distracted residence, while multi-generational natives still marvel at a new thing they never realized.

Something that is slipping from common practice is preparing the body, something that is often left to funeral homes or other mortuary services. It is a profound act of love to wash a close family member's body, comb their hair, and put fresh clothes on the corpse. Not everyone is cut out for that work but it is powerful and humbling. We come face-to-face with our own mortality and the enormity of our loss as we wash those familiar hands and sponge that beloved face. In this age of green burials and home hospice, some people are choosing to reclaim these old practices.

The next part is equally unnerving for some people. When people died at home, sometimes in the bed they were born in or in which they had given birth to their children, the women tended the body as outlined above. The men of the family might have been milling planks for a coffin, constructing the box, or digging the grave in the family's burial plot. Family would be called in from far and wide and the body of the deceased would be laid on trestles in the front room or parlor so that the rest of the extended family could file through and pay their respects, speaking their final farewells. If weather permitted, flowers and other scented greenery would be heaped around to soften the occasion as well as the smell. The burial itself might take a few days to arrange and the minister would have to be fetched from wherever he (in those days always a "he") resided. The women would do yeoman's work keeping up with the meals, and neighbors would help feed the assembled crowd. Someone always sat vigil by the body—sitting up with the dead—especially at night. Many families covered the mirrors in the house and the drapes throughout the downstairs would be drawn tight across the windows. The whole house would be hushed, the feel reverential. Ideally.

I've been told the story of one of these vigils by a buddy in South Carolina. He recalls being the youngest in a large extended family and, on the death of the matriarch, everyone gathered in. There were so many people that all the bedrooms were filled and the children were put on pallets on the floor of the parlor. (*Pallet* is an old-fashioned word that means a soft layer of bedding, a pillow, and a quilt. It is not the wooden transport structure that is a shipping container foundation for heavy objects.) The trouble was Grandma was lying in state in her open wooden casket in the parlor. All the young'uns said their prayers and got tucked under warm quilts. Just as the lights were being turned out, one rascal stage-whispered, "I think I seen her move!" All hell broke loose with children screaming and grown-ups telling them all to shut up. The lights came back on and every child got a whupping, except for my friend, who was the baby of the group. He is still pretty smug about that.

At the other end of life—at birth—there would also be a job of women's work. There are many superstitions around childbirth, which even today is an activity fraught with potential disaster. The folklore centers on the woman "opening" for childbirth and the tenets of sympathetic magic required that nothing in the birthing room be tied with a hard knot. The laces on women's garments and the strings of their aprons were loosened. If a woman wore her hair braided, that was let down and undone. A cast-iron pan might be placed under the birthing bed with a sharp knife inside. Stones with naturally occurring holes would be placed in the room and outside under the window. There would be a flat stick or short piece of leather on a table by the bed for the woman to bite down on as she labored. There was and still is a significant amount of infant and mother mortality, especially in rural areas, especially among the poor and working class. In modern-day Appalachia, African-American women are more likely to die in childbirth than their white counterparts.

From birth to death and everything in between, the hardy people of this region made the best of what they were given, which includes these odd and helpful gifts of prophetic dreaming, second sight, and the rest. As we leave this chapter on food and kitchen folkways, know that there are so many other skills that can be learned and that make for a rich and varied life. There are some resources listed at the end of the book for those of you considering learning these things in more depth.

Some Witchery: Candy Spells

In some circles, I am known for the Marshmallow Hex, which is listed on the next page. It came to me after I'd heard a fascinating talk about *kolam*, a practice from the southern part of India where the woman of the house draws a pretty design in rice flower on the street or stoop in front of the front door. As insects, birds, and little creatures eat and scatter the rice flour, more and more prosperity is accrued by the household. It was a compelling talk and it got me thinking. I pondered how the theory behind kolam could be used to magical effect. The following list of spells featuring readily available (as well as some evocative old-fashioned) candies came from that contemplation of kolam.

I developed the marshmallow spell first, and it was quite successful. While traveling with a friend to a festival in Tennessee, I had a funny thought. What if you used Necco Wafers to commune with the dead and called them "Necro Wafers"? Then the game was on and the following list is the result.

Now, none of these candy spells are traditional. The old-time mountain folks didn't have many sweets. Baked goods were sweetened with honey and sorghum, white sugar being expensive. At Christmas a child might get one stick of peppermint candy and an orange in the toe of a sock. But the spells are good-natured fun and mountain folks are always in a mood for that.

I started with the idea of the candy based on its name or flavor and then considered whether to eat it or bury it, put it in a sachet, throw it in the freezer, toss it in swiftly running water, burn it, stick it with a stabbitty, or hex it and hand it over to someone else to be eaten.

Marshmallow Hex: The One That Started It All

It's designed to cut an arrogant person down to size, and to feed some critters, as kolam does. Take a plain marshmallow and write the person's name upon it. Soft pencil is best for this. Once the writing is done, pierce the marshmallow with small sticks, thorns, or toothpicks. Place it out in nature where the ants can nibble it away, bit by bit. Please place it high in the crotch of a tree limb so that rambling dogs don't choke on it Squirrels seem to nibble around the toothpicks and insects won't be affected by them.

Necco Wafers: Necro Wafers

Are you looking to revitalize your career or your love life or to bring your latent creativity "back from the dead"? Write your intention in pencil on as many candies as feels right. Wrap them in a paper sachet and then bury it in a place you love and tend, like your flower garden.

Jelly Beans: Magic Beanstalks

Remember the old story of "Jack and the Beanstalk"? Taking that as a guide, set your intention to achieve—to climb up to—your heart's desire. Bury the jelly beans in the ground three at a time in a hill, like you'd plant corn.

Chuckles: Cheer Up!

These are rubbery jelly candies in bright colors. You can create a simple working, either for you or someone else by using them. Help your sad friend to see the light side of life by writing their name on one and burying it in fertile soil.

Chocolate Coins: Gold Ones for Sympathetic Magic

At the beginning of December every year, I start to gather chocolate coins. I give them away at the winter solstice as a wish that the young agricultural year include sweetness, brightness, and prosperity. Throughout the year, you can find gold- and silver-colored plastic coins, especially at those stores where everything costs a dollar. I have some with four-leaf clovers on them for St. Patrick's Day and others that show up for Mardi Gras. I use these in money-drawing and resource-gathering workings.

Bonbons: Sit on the Couch and Eat Some Bonbons

These fat coconut balls are covered in a firm candy coating and come in many pastel colors. They are symbolic of leisure and decadence, as though you have no work at all. When asked if I am busy, I will sometimes remark, sarcastically, naw, I've been spending all time my sitting on the couch, eating bonbons from a cut crystal bowl. But that gave me the idea for another sort of calling-in working. If you are too busy, doing way too much, too many plates spinning (or whatever symbol you use), first you should identify what you can reasonably remove from your plate of busyness and consider how you can be better about your personal boundaries. Then support your intentions with a little job of work. Take a few of those pretty little bonbons and set them out on your working area (whether desk or dining room table) on a reflective surface like a small mirror. As the moon is waxing to full, set the intention to call some leisure time your way. For extra fun, put those candies on a little crystal plate and add a doily too.

Circus Peanuts: Sometimes It Is Your Circus and Those Are Your Monkeys

Social media memes keep reminding us that we are not responsible for every little thing by blithely announcing that "this" isn't your circus or your monkeys. But sometimes it is your circus and you need to manage the mess. Use these orange puffy candies to gather in your monkeys and organize your circus. Use them in a summoning spell to bring your circus to heel and get the darn thing on the road again.

Swedish Fish: For Catching What You Need

These are the candy I most often recommend to people for connecting with the land spirits. They are easy to find and everyone knows what they look like. They come in colors other than red, but we think of them as red. What do you want to catch? A new job, a new place to live? Let each of these fish be the catch that you've reeled in, making your life a little sweeter.

Candy Pumpkins: Think of It as a Bag of Time

Pumpkins get carved up at Halloween to be jolly jack-o'-lanterns on fall-decorated front porches. If you are like most people in the modern world, one of the things you could probably use is the chance to carve out some time for what you need to do or be. Use those candy pumpkins one by one to buy yourself some time. Eat them and claim your time or bury them and do likewise.

Chapter 6
Healing and Herb Lore

From the rivers to the ridgelines, this old place continues to delight and confound those who come to it to absorb its magic and indulge in its healing, which is legendary. There are still old tuberculosis (TB) sanitariums throughout the area because doctors encouraged TB sufferers to come to the mountains for the good air and the cool summers. I was born in a Seventh-Day Adventist sanitarium with a hospital unit in west Buncombe County. The current Veterans Administration Hospital in Oteen, North Carolina, was once the site of a large TB sanitarium. Some of the original buildings remain from those old days. When antibiotics came on the scene, the mountains here lost their reputation for a magical cure.

It is one of the great quests of any age—finding techniques and materials to effect healing in the body and spirit of our human family. In a culture dominated by Protestant Christianity, we'll begin by looking at the healing power that comes from a personal relationship with the Divine, first through prayer and then through the healer's body as a vessel for the holy powers, as a vessel for the Holy Spirit to work.

We like to think of healing as removing sickness from a body, mind, or soul. To be healed is to be made whole. That is the ideal: whether through prayer, medication, or herbal treatment, the illness is made to leave the body. But sometimes healing a situation happens through more extreme means: through amputation or debilitating chemotherapy and radiation. And sometimes healing comes through the doorway of death. To make a person whole requires us to widen our view of what healing is and the ways it can be accessed and applied. In the traditionally remote parts of Appalachia, the healing techniques that were used on humans were often the same ones used for sick or injured farm animals.

If you are a theist of any sort, you are familiar with the idea of entreating the Divine you honor to bring healing. Prayer in all its forms is one form of that profound communication. Prayer is often modified to allow the Divine to do the best thing, something that we as mortal supplicants may not know, as in "Thy will, not mine, be done."

These old-style mountain healers were aware that they were vessels for heavenly power, that the skills that were brought to bear for healing came through the healer's body from a pure and holy source. This led to the commonly expressed humility, the healer being fully aware that their hands were merely tools for this power. This attitude prevails among modern practitioners, regardless of their religious or spiritual tradition.

Laying on Hands

There are many world traditions of infusing a sick person with "healing energy" from a source other than that of the healer. Reiki is the one that is familiar to most people. This healing technique involves the healer opening themselves to the spirit of healing, however they choose to name that—Holy Spirit, earth energy, Jesus, Mary. The energy is believed to enter the body of the healer and is dispersed through their hands into the sick person.

Try this exercise:

Ground yourself deeply by whatever means is your preferred one. With each inhale of breath, pull the energy from the earth up through your feet and imagine it flowing up through your body until it reaches your hands. Lay your hands directly on the ill person or directly above them, if they cannot be physically touched. Allow the energy to continue to flow up and through with every intake of breath until you get a sense of pushback from the energy of the ill person. Remove your hands slowly, allow the energy to flow down from your hands, through your body, and back into the earth. Give yourself a few moments of deep breathing and expression of gratitude, then release your grounding. It's always wise to drink some water and have a bite of food to complete your cycle of healing.

Power in the Blood

Throughout the world's history, we have known the power of blood. Menstrual blood, birth blood, sacrificial blood—the red life force that flows through all the denizens of the animal kingdom. The red dirt called ocher is a substitute for literal blood, used in prehistorical burials, and I sometimes use it and garnet as a substitute for blood when that ingredient would be useful but is not practical or appropriate.

There's an old hymn that includes the line "there is power, power, wonder-working power / In the blood of the Lamb."[15] The

---

15. Lewis E. Jones, "There Is Power in the Blood," 1899, https://hymnary.org /text/would_you_be_free_from_the_burden_jones.

song refers to the sacrifice Jesus made to save us from sin, as any mountain child—even an unchurched one like myself—knew. But the song is absolutely right: blood is life and when a job of work requires the addition of extra power, blood is often used. It can come from sticking your finger or from menstrual blood, if that is available.

Red garnets travel well and aren't messy. I use them in paper spells and in asfidity bags, both of which we'll review in a later chapter. I have used them to stop a flow of blood—as the well-known Ezekiel verse is used: "But when I passed by thee, and saw thee polluted in thine own blood, I said unto thee *when thou wast* in thy blood, Live, yea, I said unto thee *when thou wast* in thy blood, Live."[16] That verse is commonly used and comes from the Old Testament. By now you well know that the version of the Bible most used in the southern Appalachians is the one commissioned by King James I, called the KJV for short.

When you consider the possible meanings of this verse, as I did, it is remarkably difficult to understand. The repetitive phrases are intriguing, though—in thine own blood, in thy blood, in thy blood—and may be the reason it works magically.

I tried this for the first time a few years ago and the silent repetition of those three phrases did the trick. Feeling somehow bound by the notion that I was never formally taught this healing, I'd never done it before. Tradition has it that these workings must be passed down from mother to son or father to daughter, each generation taught by the opposite sex of the previous generation.

After years of experimentation, I have come to the conclusion that this is not always the case, for this or other workings. I did not learn this directly from my grandfather, though he was certainly

16. Ezekiel 16:6 (KJV).

the source for it. If we stretch the notion of "taught" to make it "source," it does still work. It requires a bit of folkloric gymnastics, but that is sometimes how folkways work. As with all things magical, I suggest you try workings that serve or interest you first and see if they work. Try it a few times before you decide whether or not it is valuable to you and then add it to your work basket.

There is a similar working that I've developed for bruises. According to some now-dead family elders, I have a percentage of "Virginia blue blood" in my genetically peasant veins. This was supposed to explain why I have always bruised easily. I mostly don't notice them unless they are particularly dramatic and draw attention from concerned friends. I may slap a cotton pad sopping with witch hazel on it and then move on. When I get a big whack or walk into the corner of something, I do an intervention based on the Ezekiel verse. I place my hand—preferably my strong (dominant) hand—gently on the bump and repeat silently: "Flow, my blood, flow around." I ground myself and speak the charm into the affected area, then repeat it twice. It usually works to lessen the colorful effect on my pale skin.

Handling fire sometimes leads to a burn, as can removing bread or pizza from the oven. There is a beautiful little spell for soothing a burn, one I saw practiced years ago and relearned from my now-deceased friend Kythryn. It is traditionally Appalachian and includes a phrase spoken three times. As always, you ground yourself into the energy of the land and pull earth energy up through your body and into your hands. Place your strong hand palm down over the afflicted area, being careful not to touch it. Move your hand in a clockwise circular motion over the burn, saying, "Come three angels from the North; take both fire and frost!" three times. You may repeat the action and the spoken charm three times if that feels correct to you.

Different parts of Appalachia have different versions of the charm. Sometimes the angels take the fire and leave the frost. Sometimes the three helpers are brides, not angels. Which leads this forensic folklorist to wonder—was this charm originally from Britain, where the healing saint and goddess Brigid is sometimes called Bride? Perhaps.

Herbal Allies

Much of my teaching over the years has been aimed at coming into relationship with the natural world. Now we will look at some green allies—plants in this region that are useful for magic as well as medicine. But instead of approaching them as a means to your end, we'll consider that a relationship is a foundational part of dealing with living beings that are part of the world in which we live.

Start simply. Wherever you live, there are green and growing things—even if they are the houseplants that freshen the air in your apartment. Love it with all you've got, that sliver of green. Learn all you can about it, as you would any new love. Is it an annual or a perennial—will it die at the end of the growing season or go dormant to reappear in spring? Is it evergreen? Where does it originate—is it native to your area or an exotic transplant?

Then widen your vision. Find another plant to learn, to befriend.

Here are some of the plants used in the folk magic I practice, a few of my favorite green things.

Blackberry
Rubus fruticosus

Blackberries belong to the class of plants called brambles, another lovely old word. Blackberry is a cousin to raspberry, another favorite for its medicinal uses as well as for the delicious jams and jellies that grace our hot-from-the-oven biscuits. Blackberry has many cultivated forms, which have larger fruit and fewer prickles than the wild variety. Berry picking is a popular pastime in the late summer and early fall, and there is always a competition to see how many gallons can be brought home to process. Blackberries are in the same family as roses, and that is obvious when you see the flowers in the spring. The plant is a perennial and considered invasive in many places. If you recall the old tale of "Sleeping Beauty," you may remember that the castle gets covered with an impenetrable thicket of thorny brambles, a forest that must be negotiated in order to reach the Beauty. Imagine that happening on untended land and you will see why some people object to it. I suspect goats will eat the leaves and younger canes because they will eat almost anything, but you may need to go behind them and hack back the old woody canes if you really want the area cleared.

The leaves and roots are sovereign for teas and tinctures that are said to reduce inflammation and help with wound healing. The best use of blackberry, as far as I am concerned, is as a diarrhea treatment in the form of blackberry jelly. Yes, plain old sugar-pectin-blackberry jelly. I now travel with little containers of the stuff because I got caught without it a few years ago, and it was not a pleasant business. I was teaching at a national Pagan festival at one of the hottest times of the year. There was no place to cool down and the heat index was 109 degrees Fahrenheit for several days in a row. The food on offer was not the healthiest, and I found myself stricken with persistent diarrhea. Rest, clean water, and the judicious use of an over-the-counter medicine finally helped, but I'm sure I could have gotten to that place sooner with a jar of blackberry jelly. Give it a try the next time you have that kind of tummy trouble and see how it works for you. Most people in this region swear by it and keep a medicinal jar in the pantry. Keep one for medicine and another for biscuits.

Bloodroot
Sanguinaria canadensis

Bloodroot's sweet late winter flower, a little white daisy, belies the skin-gnawing quality of its harvested root. The sap has been used for centuries to remove warts and skin tags and will also remove healthy flesh if used incautiously.

The pure white flowers of this native wild plant appear early in the spring, stark among last season's leaves. It grows in naturally occurring clumps and is a beacon of the coming spring. Its simplicity belies the authority, as well as the color, of the root. Its Latin name tells the story, as they often do. *Sanguinaria* means blood, and a tincture of this root is used as a remedy for warts, skin tags, and skin cancers. As I've mentioned elsewhere, there are folks here in the southern Appalachians who can rub or talk away warts. I had a great-aunt who could do that but I do not have that gift. When my daughter got warts on her hand, we tried everything from duct tape to over-the-counter products to a dermatologist. They just kept coming back. I wished, not for the first time, for my great-aunt's gift. As a result of her visit to the school nurse at her college, we tried bloodroot tincture and that did the trick. Since that time, I've recommended it to many people, all of whom have met with good success. You can dig and tincture it yourself, but a good health food store or food co-op can order it for you, if they don't stock it.

Catnip
Nepeta cataria

There is no question that catnip is a drug, especially for cats. And an otherwise aloof and docile kitty will soon be mewing, rolling on its back, and napping in the garden. The cat that lives next door ate my catnip to the ground, and I had to cover it with a metal mesh box to save it from too much affection.

Catnip holds an interesting place in my personal—and in regional—history. It was believed to prevent internal hives in babies: a concern among mountain folks until very recently. At the first sign of discomfort, a mother was told to feed the infant strong catnip tea. Catnip is a soporific herb, causing drowsiness. It also helps relieve colic pains and helps babies pass painful gas. The mother would sip the tea as she fed it to the baby and both parties would relax a bit. Over time and with consistent use, the mother's milk came down better and the baby's tummy began to feel more settled. What was called "hives" wouldn't break out and all would be well. This was true when I was growing up, but I haven't heard it recently. Again, it is a folkloric use and a parent should check with the child's pediatrician before using any herbal products.

Chickweed
Stellaria media

Chickweed appears in moist areas in the early spring. It is bright green and tastes like cornsilk smells. It can be eaten out of hand—I go a little mad when I first see it in the spring. I will sometimes get down on my hands and knees and graze through a clump of it. But more often I pick it and give it a good rinsing when I get home. It is good in salads and makes a rich pesto sauce when blended with a little olive oil, salt, and a dab of lemon juice.

It is used medicinally as a tea and is said to be good for the kidneys (it is a gentle diuretic), relieves pain, treats conjunctivitis (what we call pink eye), and can be mashed up and applied as a poultice to help remove splinters. Some folks smoke the dried plant to aid in asthma treatment. In my experience, plain white potatoes grated and applied as a poultice work better for splinters. But I do find chickweed tea to be mildly diuretic and delicious. I prefer it as a wild food—it tastes like the best of summer and comes to light in the early spring, when my heart and my tummy need it the most.

Chickens also love it, hence the name. If you have a hungry flock of these charming, useful critters, you may have to fight them for the chickweed. Or gather plenty of it where and as you can and share it with your "girls." All of you will be happy about that.

Dandelion
Taraxacum officinale

Coffee is ubiquitous in the modern world, and it is hard to imagine a world without a coffee shop on every corner. Years ago, a nice strong brew was concocted from roasted dandelion and chicory root because coffee was either unavailable or too dear. You can get both in your local herb shop or can dig and roast the roots yourself, though I have never done so. This beverage is bitter, answering our human need for that astringent taste. I like it with some cream to soften the sharpness. It is good and a different way to start your day or perk up your afternoon. No caffeine too.

Dandelions are the weed everyone loves to hate, or so you'd suspect if you visit your local garden center. Dandelion greens are nutritious and delicious. Simply pull or cut the young leaves, wash them thoroughly, and sauté them in a little olive oil with a sprinkle of salt. They are cut-and-come-again plants. The more you harvest them, the more they produce. Young and tender leaves are the most flavorful, but even the older leaves are good, if you don't mind a little bitterness. They are good in omelets too.

Dandelion, like all the green world, is filled with profound and simple magic. It is green and golden and white and the seeds are natural wish-bringers. What child doesn't know to wish on the fluffy seed head and then blow all those seeds into the sky? In addition to all the drinks and foods this wonderful plant can be used in, I use it magically to help make dreams come true and to help clients find ways to know their heart's true desire.

Elderberry (Black)
Sambucus nigra

I am an elderberry evangelist and am not the only one. I can't remember where or from whom I first learned the properties of elderberry but I have been using it for a long time and experiment with it to see what else it can do. One of the great gifts of the elderberry is her generosity: she makes enough blossom in the spring so that we may take some to use as medicine, in case the berries never form. I have found you can easily have both, if you are careful. I usually tincture the berries—either fresh or dried—in rum or gin.

In a year when there is a prolific elderberry flowering, you can easily take half the flowers for cordials. Since I am by nature an omen and sign reader, I usually equate a heavy elderberry harvest with a potentially nasty cold and flu season on the horizon. This year I harvested enough of the blossom to create an elderberry cordial and left the rest for making berries, which the birds stole before I could harvest them. And in a good year, like this one, there is a blessed sufficiency.

Horehound
Marrubium vulgare

It looms so large in my memory, this raucous perennial herb. It can usually be found lounging around my garden, spreading itself languidly into places it shouldn't go. Bees and other pollinators love its flowers, and its strange scent lingers in the air when you brush past it on your way to somewhere else. It has been recorded as a medicinal herb since the first century BCE.

Horehound is part of my family legend too. My great-grandmother—my mother's mother's mother-in-law—was born before the Civil War and lived to be 106. She was "pure Irish," according to the family—a black-haired beauty who married a man with whom she had my grandfather and later married a man who gave her more sons, including my much-loved Uncle John, with whom she lived in her advanced age. There is no mention of a divorce from the first husband, a rambling man who may have been a Traveler.

I remember her as a tiny woman who mostly sat in a ladder-backed chair outside the door of her little house. She showed me the best way to kill a chicken for dinner and her movements were sure and practiced. She chuck-cucked to the little flock and threw out some crumbs from her apron pocket. Her bony arm swept down upon the chosen sacrifice, picking it up by the head. She twisted it around hard and carried it a little distance to a wooden block. She picked up the hatchet there and flipped the limp bird down. In a flash, she chopped off its head and grabbed it up by the feet, careful to not get any blood on her. The little head lay on the wooden surface, its beak opening and closing. She stood there until her daughter-in-law took the bird from her and went away to her own kitchen. My Irish great-grandmother leaned her hand on my shoulder and we went back to her chair. She sat down lightly, dusted her hands on her apron, and handed me a hard candy from her apron pocket. I secretly wiped it on my shirt and popped it into my mouth. She took one herself and we spent some time watching the chickens adjust themselves and go back to their usual routine, as though nothing had happened.

The family proudly claims that she lived the last ten years of her life in that little house, eating nothing but cooked pork fat and horehound candy and drinking nothing but Coca-Cola. Ten years. It was a long, mysterious, and happy life and in my mind's eye, it is forever perfumed with horehound candy and sweet snuff.

Many marvelous things are attributed to horehound, including strengthening the immune system, lowering cholesterol, and managing blood glucose levels, among many others. If even half of these miracles are half true, I have to wonder how much it contributed to her longevity. It may have been genetics, but I like to think all those little horehound candies helped.

Mugwort
Artemisia vulgaris

This big fragrant herb is one of the ones I go to first, time and again. It has a broad and untidy growing habit, resembling a chrysanthemum. Its scent is as strong as a mum's too. It grows in all sorts of wild places, often on the edges of parks and parking lots, close to humans. It is commonly called mugwort because it was used to make beer before the introduction of hops. This style of beer (ale, usually) is called gruit. I have made a mugwort and sorghum ale that is light in alcohol and warming in the belly. Mugwort is a wonderful weed that can be drunk as a tea, brewed into a light alcohol ale, and burned as sacred smoke. It has long been known as a dream tonic. A person suffering from nightmares and even night terrors can benefit from using mugwort. The herb brings your dreams down to a manageable level. It clears the path for more recollection if you don't remember your dreams. It also aids in deep sleeping. I use it dried in sachets and have clients put the sachet inside their pillow. But I prefer it fresh and just cut. Bring a big branch in from the yard and place it inside the pillowcase and under the pillow, so that you crush it and release the scent all night long. If you are uncomfortable with that, cut shorter branches and place them in a jar of water on your bedside table. Mugwort may also be used in lucid dreaming and as an aid in trance and guided meditation.

I have found another use for this remarkable herb that I want to share with you. I and others have found it to be both calming and helpful in hospice situations, where loved ones are making the decision to go from us. Sitting by the bedside of a dying person is an intimate, soul-shaking experience. But sometimes the body is reluctant to let go of life, to let the spirit fly free. When people sadly remark on the fragility of life, I suspect they have never sat by the bedside of an elder who lingers on in pain and prays for Jesus to come and take her home. Mugwort when used in its fresh form or used as an aromatic wash can ease open the veil to the dreamtime and open the door to let that tired old soul pass through. It is a gentle but strong ally in that transition. It's the scent of it, as far as I can tell, so use fresh mugwort, cut and placed in water or make a strong tea and take cotton balls doused with it into the room where your loved one is making the final journey. Dab it on the pulse points and on the upper lip under the nose.

The genus *Artemisia* also gives us wormwood, from which we make the Green Fairy, absinthe. It is an all-around helpful herb, easy to grow, with many useful purposes.

Nota bene: Mugwort can have a mild abortifacient effect, so if you are pregnant or thinking of trying for it, don't handle the plant and certainly do not ingest it in any form.

Plantain
Plantago major or P. minor

Plantain creates great patches in the spring of the year. It is a personal favorite: a plant that grows in waste places, on the edges of gardens, and through the crack at the edge of the front stoop. It is tenacious, simple little plantain. *Plantago major* is broad-leafed plantain and it is edible, medicinal, and magical. This European native is tough and strong and is a shade of green so rich—even in poor soil, even in little soil—that you know how important it is in the scheme of things. What a rich salve this plant makes. Sometimes in conjunction with other herbs and greens, it is good for all sorts of skin ailments, from bug bites to stings to contact dermatitis from things like harvesting stinging nettles. It is important and plentiful but it isn't an orchid or an exotic sort of lily. It is a weed that people poison out of their perfect suburban lawns. It is a nutritious medicinal herb that can be sautéed for supper or chewed raw to become a poultice for an insect bite.

Poke
Phytolacca americana

Poke, poke sallet, or pokeweed is *Phytolacca americana*, a stately and vigorous plant that is common throughout much of the region. Its growth habit is tall and expansive, and the strange leathery leaves feel primitive. One of many Appalachian "spring tonic" plants, poke can be eaten in the early spring. It must be harvested when the leaves are very young, and it must be prepared carefully. Most

people don't pick poke if it's taller than seven inches, and they boil
it in two changes of water before frying it up in pork fat or butter.
In spite of the "sallet" part of its name, it is never, to my knowledge,
eaten as a raw salad.

Its vibrant autumn berries are rich and fat, and at that point
its stems and leaves are toxic. The berries are used as dye and ink.
Locally, pokeberries are said to prevent rheumatism if one berry
is eaten every day from the time they are perfectly ripe—shiny,
black, and fat with juice—until frost. I've never known anyone
who has done that, but I know lots of older women who dye their
gray hair purple every autumn, enjoying the bright color as well as
the temporary nature of this homemade hair treatment.

Queen Anne's Lace
Daucus carota

Every summer when I was a child, I was warned about Queen
Anne's lace. Filled with chiggers, everyone said. Oh, it's pretty,
but pretty is as pretty does. It is such a beautiful flower, a big head
of white lace with a tiny velvet bead in its heart. But none of us
wanted chiggers, which itched like the devil and necessitated
having each itch painted with fingernail polish so that our arms
and legs were covered in Cutex Old Rose blobs. Chiggers are tiny
insects that bite you and were believed to then burrow into your
skin, where the tormenting itching commenced.

As a woman, I often think about the harsh realities of life in a
world where you had little or no control over your reproductive life,
because the culture demanded many children and there was no way
of knowing how many would reach adulthood. Mountain women
have used—and some still use—wild carrot seed, including Queen
Anne's lace, as a birth control method, but any natural method

requires strict attention to both your body and the calendar by both parties in baby-making. The Protestant structure of family life made it near impossible for a woman to say no to her husband when it came to intimate matters. Mountain women would carefully lay these seeds by in the fall, often in the root cellar. They were inserted in the vagina after sex and acted to prevent the implantation of a fertilized egg. They were chewed and ingested to do the same thing.

I am still paranoid enough about chiggers to cut the flowers while wearing gloves. I use the seeds or complete flower heads (dried) in sachets as part of ancestor work (because of their dainty frilliness). Please be careful of those chiggers, though, or you'll wish you were an ancestor.

Rabbit Tobacco
Pseudognaphalium obtusifolium

A little something in general about herbs and their uses and names. There are words and phrases that are beautiful in their own way, words that wiggle off the tongue and into the light of day. I always recommend that you learn the botanical name of any plant you plan to work with because the common names vary from place to place and because the names themselves are so darned fun to say out loud. I have been talking about and writing about rabbit tobacco for many years. I use it as part of my Sweet Smoke blend and use it alone as a light incense, but it has many uses, medicinally and folklorically. And its Latin name is a long and winding road that I love to say aloud: *Pseudognaphalium obtusifolium*. I had about five years of Latin so it is fun for me but if you're afraid of those long words, here's a hint: break it down by syllables and pronounce most every letter. Take the second part of rabbit tobacco's name for example. *Ob-toos-uh-fo-lee-um*. It's pretty easy when you set your mind to it, and effective plant identification requires using their proper names.

The same plant can have many names—this one is also called sweet everlasting and old field balsam. And something called rabbit tobacco might be a different plant altogether, like *Anaphalis margaritacea*. So learning their formal names as you get to know them is important. Every country kid I know has tried to smoke rabbit tobacco, which, in spite of its common name, is not in the tobacco family at all. It was rumored to have an intoxicating effect, but none of us found that to be so. It is a ragged plant, prone to the edges of waste areas, like parking lots and the edges of new construction areas. I have found it very helpful as an incense that promotes both calm and relaxation, and so it is useful for meditation and trance purposes.

Most of the folkloric uses we have for this herb come from Native American peoples and early settlers. It has such a sweet and lasting smell, even after it's dried, and the Creek made it into a perfume. Some of its historic uses include as a decoction of both flowers and leaves to fight the symptoms of the common cold, for rheumatism, and as a mouthwash for gum sores.

Rue
Ruta graveolens

Rue is not native to this area and has not naturalized here, so growing your own is a good idea. Unless you know how handling the fresh plant affects your skin, please wear gloves when handling it. It can cause skin irritation (contact dermatitis) in some people. The second warning is that rue is a known abortifacient. If you are pregnant or thinking along those lines, avoid handling it altogether. Better safe than sorry. Rue oil acts as rocket fuel for any working you are concocting. That's it, really. I use it on almost everything. I use it for house blessing too.

Sour Grass/Woods Sorrel
Oxalis acetosella

We used to eat this as children and we called it "sair" grass. Much later in my life, I found the name most people know it by—woods sorrel. It is a little plant, growing close to the ground. It has shamrock-shaped leaves and bright yellow flowers on thin stalks. As the spring progresses, the yellow flowers transform into seedpods that resemble tiny okra pods. It is a prolific plant and fairly common here in the southern highlands.

We pulled it up and ate the whole thing, except the roots. It can be eaten in salads, cooked in creamy soups, or blended into a pesto-like sauce. True to its name, it is a tangy treat, however you use it. Sour grass, whether dried or fresh, also makes a delicious tea, especially when sweetened with a spoonful of honey. It is thirst-quenching, especially if you have a cold.

It can be used as a natural dye and medicinally it can be chewed, chopped, or blended for boils and abscesses. It has some diuretic and fever-reducing properties too. But mostly, it is a delicious perennial herb that appears very early in the spring.

Stinging Nettle
Urtica dioica

Stinging nettle is aptly named. Hairs on this sturdy perennial plant will sting if your flesh comes into contact with it. These hairs cover the entire plant so safely picking this important plant is best done with some long gloves and a good pair of pruners. As the plant ages, it exudes the familiar pungent odor of cat pee, making it easy to find in the wild. It is best harvested when very young and can be used as a tea and as a pot herb. Nettles grow in rich, moist soil in moist areas, near creeks and on riverbanks, at the edge of the woods and shady parking lots. I take a deep basket with me when harvesting and I wear leather and canvas rose gauntlets. At home, I wash the plant under running water, holding it with metal tongs. There is a pot of water boiling on the stove and the nettles go into that pot, the lid goes on, and the burner is turned off. I leave the nettles steeping for several hours, sometimes overnight, and drain the tea into half-gallon canning jars that go into the fridge. Some folks like to add honey while the tea is still warm but I refer it plain.

Once the plant has been submerged in boiling water, the stinging effect is neutralized. Nettles can be sautéed then, in butter and olive oil, with some chopped garlic. Stinging nettles are believed to be helpful in treating inflammation and lowering blood pressure. But most use it as a nutritious tea, good for cleansing the liver.

Sumac
Rhus glabra

I've named this familiar plant sweet sister sumac, but I grew up calling it "shoe-make." It is such a helpful plant and so beautiful. You can make a pleasantly sour "lemonade" from her berries or dry and crush them to use as a spice. The root of this good sister is antiseptic, and it is easily found in waste areas and old farmsteads. It has a tall growth habit and bears the fruit upright. Its bark has been used as a gargle for mouth ulcers and sore throats. Some Native American peoples use it for asthma and diarrhea.

Her shadow twin is *Toxicodendron vernix*, poison sumac, a plant that rivals poison ivy in its effect on bare skin. Avoid that one, please. And if you're unsure which is which, ask your friendly local herbalist to help you out with plant identification.

Vervain
Verbena hastata or V. officinalis

Vervain is one of my favorite magical plants, and I create vervain oil to use as both a dressing and an anointing oil. My favorite is V. *hastata* (blue vervain), but V. *officinalis* (common vervain) will do in a pinch.

I learned what was described to me as a Cornish weather spell that consists of half an eggshell held in the soft hand and a sprig of vervain, some whisky or cider, and your spit placed into it. The thumb of the strong hand is pressed into the center of the egg and is turned clockwise to call in a storm. I told a witch-friend near Penzance about the working and she'd never heard of it as traditionally Cornish, but I assured her it worked very well.

Given that use as a weather-working herb, I and some of my colleagues have found another use for the dressing oil made from this helpful plant. We have begun using it in our work as death midwives and grief counselors. It seems to be a helper for those who are walking through the long grief process of death or reclaiming happiness in their lives following a heartbreak, whether a breakup or job loss. Dress your choice of candle and set your intention to take advantage of this watery and soothing plant.

Witch Hazel
Hamamelis virginiana

There is an over-the-counter remedy that has been around for decades: witch hazel either distilled in alcohol or alcohol free. You have guessed by now that I was a rough-and-tumble sort of child, climbing and hiking, falling down, wrecking bikes, being stepped on by ornery ponies. The family remedy for most of those was dousing a wound with Mercurochrome or tincture methylate. But a bump on any part of the body—forehead, knee, ankle—might raise up a pumpknot and require a generous application of witch hazel, usually on a dripping cotton ball or wadded up handkerchief. It was held on the bruised place as long as I would hold still and generally helped with the ailment it was supposed to treat. I still use it for that.

We have a large Japanese witch hazel in the front yard where we can observe its strange habits. The leaves change late in the fall and they change color from near the trunk outward, bright yellow that soon turns a tannish-brown and clings stubbornly to the plant. The bush starts to release the leaves in the early winter to make room for the flowers that will appear as yellow squiggles around Yuletide. The new leaves come in months later, after the sweet blossoms. Another strange thing is the fat and knobbed seedpod that explodes when it's ready and sends pointy black seeds as far from the mother plant as possible.

I buy witch hazel in a bottle for my bump-knots and bruises but use those stubborn leaves magically to steady myself when a project or situation requires tenacity, which is a polite way to say stubbornness. I pile them in a bowl on my worktable or altar and wrap them into bundles, tying the bundle with embroidery floss in a bright and lively green. I've also written intentions directly on the leaves with a black marker and left the little bundles in places that feel right for the intention. I dry the new leaves, after the plant has flowered, and I use them in sachets to bring the client clarity and wisdom.

Poisonous Plants and Their Uses

The herbs, oils, remedies, and the like contained within these pages are
offered as a representation of traditional folklore and are not intended to
diagnose or cure any conditions or diseases

Poisonous plants are very popular these days, with websites and
blogs devoted to their cultivation and potential uses. There is a particular fascination with "flying ointments," which are not part of
mountain magic, or at least the mountain magic that I know and
practice.

Let's spend a moment contemplating the uses of plants that
are healing as well as toxic, bearing out the old axiom about healing and hexing occupying opposite sides of the same disk. We
will honor the dance of bane and wort, potent allies in the work
of herbalist and witch and wise woman. Many Pagans and witches
are excited to grow a garden of poisonous plants, and you may
choose to do the same. These plants are bold and dramatic and are
a striking addition to a flower or herb garden. We will focus on the
medicinal and magical properties of the plants and ponder their
history and place in local lore and in mountain myth.

Angel Trumpet
Datura stramonium

What a gorgeous flower! The original is creamy white, but hybrid
versions are white with a purple throat or ruffled or blush-rose or
a splendid gold. All are very poisonous. The plants tend to spread
themselves around pastures and fence lines. It's also called thorn
apple and jimsonweed. It should be pulled from pastures, by the
way. Cows and horses will nibble it, to their detriment. The seedpods are fat balls with spikes, and when ready they split apart at

the tip to reveal row upon row of flat seeds. It is a large and hand-some plant but every part of it is poisonous. Don't handle it without gloves. I use those seedpods in workings that require strength and intense purpose, inserting them into sachets and being very careful that no one can access the finished spell.

Foxglove
Digitalis purpurea

Every fairy garden should have great stands of foxglove in the corners and around the little pond. It is an old-fashioned garden favorite and is also the source of digitalis, a heart drug. I use the leaves and flowers as a lure and a talisman when working with land spirits.

Nightshade
Atropa belladonna

Ah, the delicious and deadly nightshades! Tomatoes, potatoes, egg-plant, peppers—all belong to Solanaceae, the nightshade family of plants. Many of them are edible and comprise a big portion of the Appalachian diet. But Atropa is not edible and shouldn't be handled carelessly. It is a scraggly plant, but the dark, almost black berries are dramatic and beautiful. I have an Atropa in the side yard, and I use its leaves for protective magic.

Henbane
Hyoscyamus niger

Henbane is hard to grow in the moist soil of the southern hills. It is prone to flea beetles, but it has a pretty flower. It has an ancient lineage as a witch plant. I have tried to grow it in my own yard and haven't had any luck with the finicky thing. I have used a gift of henbane leaves in a sachet to encourage a mild person to be brave and to ask for what they need.

Mountain Laurel
Kalmia latifolia

The mountains here seem to come alive in the spring with the bloom of mountain laurel that runs from hill to hill in big patches that are called, appropriately enough, laurel "hells." Inexperienced hikers get lost in these thickets and sometimes never get out. I was always taught that burning the leaves or branches of this *Kalmia* produces toxic smoke, but there is some question about the truth of that. In the "better safe than sorry" department, I am going to leave that question to others and continue to refrain from burning it. Mountain laurel is often on my home altar as a tribute to these old mountains and my people here.

Mayapple
Podophyllum peltatum

These are big bright plants and easy to identify in the woods. Every part of it is toxic, though the little fruit that ripens in July is sometimes eaten. I don't recommend it, as too much of it will make you very sick indeed. It is sometimes called American mandrake, but the two plants are not related. Some herbalists use a preparation of its leaves to remove warts and skin tags, in the same way that bloodroot is used. It is a beautiful plant for a shady garden and, under proper growing conditions, makes a sizeable colony.

I have used the green fruit—did I mention it's toxic?—when the job of work requires that the client's tormentor or stalker be pushed away.

Some Witchery: Bindings

Folk magic of whatever kind is full of interference in other lives and that's the truth of it. Sometimes that interference is kindly, like the insistent, repeated advice from your best friend. Sometimes it is unwholesome and meddling. In either case, there are all sorts of simple and homely techniques that are used to heal or otherwise change a situation or person's behavior.

In my teaching on banework (I offer workshops and retreats on topics of "willful bane") and in consultations with clients, I will often offer binding techniques as a simple way to correct a situation. Let me hasten to say that a binding does not bind you to the subject of the binding. You are employing a magical technique and standing back. *Binding* refers to the act of hindering the actions of another person. You can bind yourself too. If you want to stop smoking or biting your nails, you can do a binding spell to help you on your way.

There are several techniques that are traditional to Appalachian folk magic. My favorite is the egg binding. You will need a raw egg still in its shell, a length of twine or string, and a pencil with soft lead. You can use any string, yarn, or ribbon, but please be sure it is natural and will decompose when left in weather. No plastic, no polyester. Cotton and wool are best.

Ground yourself and breathe yourself into a receptive state of mind. Ponder the working ahead of you. Take into account the situation, the people involved, your prejudice for or against one of the parties, and whether you are undertaking a grudge match with someone you don't like. If you are approaching the work as a way to heal a person or situation and feel clear about what your involvement really is in the situation in question, proceed to do the binding. When I was coming up, we used the sisal rope called binders twine that was used to tie up hay bales.

Drawing energy through your body and into your hands, focus on the job of work in front of you. Call to your mind's eye the face of the subject to be bound. State your intention aloud or to yourself. Write the person's name directly on the eggshell while considering the intention. Keep writing the name and intention on the egg until there is no clean eggshell left. Now take up your length of twine.

Holding a three-inch tail of the twine with your soft thumb, begin wrapping the egg slowly, again stating the intention. Cover the entire egg, which will now resemble a ball of twine. As you finish covering it, make sure to leave another length of twine near the tail under your thumb to tie off the entire working. Tie the two ends together with as many knots as feel right to you, setting the working into motion. You may choose to say words at the end, something like "and so it is" or "all done." I put the whole shebang into the freezer for a moon cycle. When I remove it from the freezer, I either bury it off my land or throw it into swiftly running water—a river, not a creek.

You can do a similar working with a short, stout stick—what is called a "staub" around these parts. The name is carved onto the stick and the stick wrapped accordingly, setting your intention into the tool. Then the stick is burned, thrown into that same river, or dropped into the outhouse, if you have one. That last part is traditional but I hope you have a nice flush toilet, if that is your choice.

The third binding technique is to put a photograph into a plastic bag and place the whole thing in the freezer. This is not traditional, of course, and I find it to be ineffective.

As always, if you are not called to do this sort of direct-action magic that is so much a part of folk magic don't force yourself to do it. It should be undertaken as a way to make things better, not to get back at someone or be an agent of justice. Let Justice do her own work and you do yours.

Chapter 7

Signs and Omens

This chapter is itself a compendium of information about divination and reading the signs. Betwixt the good earth and the blue sky, there are many things that influence the lives of the people in southern Appalachia. We are going to start with divination and reading omens, grounded in the thin soil, and surge upward to consider the effects of the moon and other planets on planting procedures and magical techniques in the region. There are techniques that are practiced here, including tea leaf and coffee grounds reading, scrying, and cartomancy (card reading).

As we explored in the previous chapter, the folk magic of this region is often concerned with healing, whether ailments or situations, and also with what the future will bring, which is determined by reading signs and omens, and consulting different forms of divination. That's probably true of most folk magics. When I teach about these folkways, I frequently say that clients' needs fall into a few simple categories—resources, luck, health, love, and justice/revenge. It's a helpful grouping for discerning what's what and whether you can help.

I encounter this so often and I don't have a name for this set of esoteric skills, skills that seem to be inherited in some way. They include prophetic dreams, hands-on healing, second sight, overlooking (a kind of remote viewing), and seeing the dead and hearing their voices. We discussed the Scots-Irish and some of the seemingly natural gifts that flow into their Appalachian descendants. When I was growing up, I was told that when I became a woman (had my first menstrual period), I'd inherit one of the family gifts. I'm not the only one to be told this in that way, and ours is not the only family to pass this down—far from it.

Once a young woman I didn't know sat down opposite me for a tarot reading. As is my custom, I asked her what she was looking for. I listened as I shuffled the cards and laid them out, facedown. She answered in a quiet voice. I want to know if I'm crazy. I looked up then into her pale, strained face. She told me she knew things she shouldn't know, that she saw ghosts and heard their voices. I held out both my hands and she gripped them tightly. Where are your people from? I asked. McDowell County, she replied. Before that? The answer was evident in her milk-white skin and auburn hair. My people are English and Scotch-Irish. I squeezed her hands, asked her to take a deep breath, and then told her what her family should have told her years before, about those peculiar skills that often manifest in the descendants of Scots-Irish and Scottish immigrants.

I was angry on her behalf and for all the descendants of immigrants who brought more than hopes and dreams to their new country. Skills that their Christian families are often terrified and suspicious of, assuming them to be "of the devil." And instead of encouraging these helpful, often practical, abilities, those who exhibit them are punished, shunned, and terrorized in order to save their souls. These children are never told about their great-aunt and how she knew all the news before anyone else in a way that honored her. Instead they're excused as the weird or tetched relative, belittled, betrayed. I talk to people across the Appalachian diaspora who shut down their gifts in order to stop the parental censure, only to discover that their grandmother had the same abilities, that it runs in the family. I was lucky, possibly because my parents weren't religious is any recognizable way. I was told about it in a perfectly natural way and it became a perfectly natural part of my life as I grew up. I did the same for my daughter, and one day, if she chooses to, she will pass the information on to her children.

Prophetic Dreaming

Prophetic dreaming includes dreams of events that later come to pass and recurring dreams that warn of danger. The latter vary person to person, and tradition tells us that the content of the dream must never be shared or the gift will be lost. These are the dreams my grandmother had, the ones that colored my childhood. I also have them but irregularly.

Second Sight

Second sight is popular in fiction and film. It is also called "knowing" or "having a knowing" about a person or event. It is also well documented in folklore circles. In Gaeilge, it is *an da shealladh* or *d-shealladh*, which means "two-sighted." In my experience, second sight begins at the first signs of puberty when it joins other confusing physical issues. It sometimes manifests sporadically and usually includes foreknowledge of an immediate event. You're walking in the city with your kid, starting to cross the street, and she pulls you back onto the sidewalk just as a car runs the red light. It could be a coincidence, but it should pique your interest. It may seem like a difficult conversation with a child but your honesty and care will help them deal with a gift that is useful but too often misunderstood. It will help them understand that they aren't "crazy." We've given a whole new spin on the concept of "the talk." You can do it. Be gentle and share what you know.

Some of these gifts are forbidden by some of the religious groups in the area, groups that view them as demonic and anti-Christian. There are families that practice these skills quietly and avoid public rebuke. In any case, the skills are useful and traditionally practiced by the people here.

Overlooking, or Remote Viewing

I've been thinking about what I learned as a youngster about "overlooking" and sometimes "looking over"—a remote viewing technique that I've tried with some success. The point is to check out what someone is up to though they are physically far from you. It was years later I discovered that it was also called remote viewing. In this age of video chat, it seems so unnecessary. But it's an elegant nod to old traditional ways and you may want to give it a try.

Here is the technique I learned and the one I use. Set up a mirror on a sturdy table so that it sits at a slight angle away from you as you sit. Put a medium-size taper candle in a low candle holder and light it, allowing the flame to settle. Turn off the lights so that the room is dark except for the light of the taper. You'll see the flame, reflected in the mirror, as well as your face lit by the candle. Look away from the actual flame and focus on its reflection, the candle in the mirror. Breathe your way to some quietude. Breathe. Breathe. Look past the candle in the mirror and into the reflection of the darkened room. Bring to your mind the place or person you want to observe. In your mind's eye, trace the features of the face or location. Keep breathing as your eyes search the darkness in the mirror. You may need to focus on a particular aspect in order to connect in—your daughter's braided hair, your mother's hands. When you start to bring that into view, you can begin to build the rest of your loved one and then watch what they're doing. Start with a short session but expect that most sessions should be brief, no more than fifteen minutes. You can adjust the placement of the candle and the mirror as you tune in, and it sometimes helps to unfocus your eyes. This technique was popular with mothers who continued to live in the homeplace after the children had moved into town for work or marriage.

Cartomancy

Reading cards has been a hushed-up activity for a long time here, mostly because strong Baptists find playing cards a gateway to worse vices. So there were folks, mostly women, in my experience, who squirreled away a battered deck of playing cards that were never used for card games because that was dangerous. I learned this method of cartomancy early on before I got a partial tarot deck (major arcana only) in a book from a Scholastic book fair in junior high school. It is a handy skill to have and was often used to see how an illness would go or if a love match would prosper. The cards are usually wrapped in a piece of pretty cloth, like a linen hanky, and tucked away in a drawer until needed. I never knew anyone who had a particular layout for a reading, like we do today. The cards were mixed up or shuffled briefly and several cards laid out in a row on the table.

The first time this was done for me, a neighbor sat me down at her little table and went to get the cards. There was a question she needed answered about a family member and this seemed the best way to go about that. She came back to the table, unwrapped the little deck and shuffled it twice. Slowly she laid out the cards, going from right to left. Eight cards were carefully settled, one after another and faceup. She wrapped the rest of the deck and sat back with her hands resting on the edge of the table. She studied the message and nodded, having gotten her answer. She told me what each suit meant. Hearts are for love and family, spades for health and death, diamonds for money and luck, and clubs for work. Any reversed cards were turned right-side up, as I recall. When the answer was clear, the cards were rewrapped and carefully put back into that dark drawer until they were needed again.

Scrying Methods

I taught myself tea leaf reading, though it is traditional in these parts. The technique involves using loose tea and using the dregs of it for divination purposes. Warm your teapot and make sure your tea water comes to a full boil. Choose the tea that suits your fancy and use a palmful for each cup in the pot. If you've warmed your pot by filling it with hot water, dump the water out and throw the loose leaves in. Pour boiling water onto the leaves and allow the tea to steep to the desired strength. Enjoy it with a friend by pouring the steeped tea through a strainer and into cups. At the end of the pot, bypass the strainer and pour the tea dregs into each cup. Sip away as much of the tea as possible and pour the wet dregs onto a saucer. Swirl it around a little and look at the patterns the dregs make in the saucer. You can use the symbols for reading playing cards as a guide. Do the tea leaves look like a heart? Love and family. You get the drift. There are common symbols for everyday things, but it's best if you decide what those symbols mean to you. It looks like a tree—what do trees mean to you? Your love of nature or your need to be there more often perhaps?

Coffee grounds are done the same way. You can use a French press to brew your coffee, and be sure to leave a little coffee in the press so that it pours onto your saucer easily. Then scry those squiggles and see what your drink is telling you about your life and your future.

There is a small cast-iron frying pan that hangs on the pot rack with my other cookware. Too small for much except melting butter or frying up one egg. It's well seasoned, of course, as any cast-iron cookware should be in an Appalachian kitchen. But I don't use it for cooking. I put a cup of water in it, light a candle, and turn off the overhead light in the kitchen. Then I use it as a scrying mirror. People use scrying, as they do overlooking, for a variety of things, but mostly it's a predictive tool. This is not traditional—as far as I know I invented it and yet I can see our foremothers gazing into a pan of water on the cookstove and peering into the future. There are many tools for scrying and many ways to do it, but I love my little cast-iron scrying pan.

On my way to a speaking and teaching engagement in upstate New York, I stopped overnight in a funky roadside motel. It was neither clean nor well furnished, but it was cheap. Next morning I checked out and the surly front desk clerk mentioned a current event that was puzzling to her. I shrugged and said I would get my cards out later and see what was going on. Her entire demeanor changed and she grinned at me. "You read tarot?"

Tarot rhymed with *carrot* but I nodded yes. She yelled for someone in the back room, who appeared in the doorway, as sullen as the clerk had been. "This lady here reads tarot!" Again, that change.

The second woman was, as they say, great with child. "Can you tell if it's a boy or a girl?"

"She don't have her cards."

"Yeah, but can you tell?"

I put down my bag. "Have you done the wedding ring on a string?"

"No, we did a pencil and thread."

I looked at her and she was carrying high, which usually means a girl in mountain lore. The woman was sad. She really wanted a boy because her husband didn't have a son, only daughters.

I tell this story to introduce another reason that foretelling, or *bodement* (which is another traditional word for this), was traditionally employed—determining the sex of an unborn child. There are signs that are sometimes accurate. If pregnancy sickness happens in the morning, it's likely a boy. If pregnancy sickness happens in the afternoon, it's likely to be a girl. If the pregnancy brings the joy of heartburn, the baby will be born with a full head of hair.

Some of you are probably familiar with the idea of a baby born with a veil, or caul, over the face. It is a piece of amniotic sac that's present on the face or head of a newborn child. A child born with this is thought to be born lucky and to have special abilities, including communing with the dead and second sight.

In a life bound by the strictures of birth, upbringing and religion, a mountain native was often eager to find out about the future to look forward to anticipating something wonderful or to prepare for a challenging event. There is an old mountain superstition about marriage that I have experienced. If someone sweeps under your feet while you are sitting down, you will never marry. I know for a fact that this isn't a true thing because I stuck my feet out every time my mother swept where I was sitting reading. She dutifully swept underneath them—but I have been married now for thirty-three years.

Weather

In a land of subsistence farming, knowing the weather is vital to surviving. Predicting the extent of winter weather gives an idea of how much preparation is needed—wood for heating, hunting, preserving food, and the like. In the fall of the year, and starting as early as August, we count how many mornings begin in fog. Some folks keep a jar of beans, adding a bean for every misty morning. At the end of August, you count the beans and know how many snows there may be in the coming winter season.

The appearance of woolly worms is always a cause for strict attention. They are the caterpillar for the Isabella tiger moth (*Pyrrharctia isabella*) and are usually reddish-brown in the middle and black on either end. The width of the black bands indicates the extent and severity of winter weather. More black means a harsher winter. These little critters seem to be everywhere in the fall of the year as they poke around for a safe place to overwinter. There are thirteen body segments on these fine fellers and thirteen weeks of winter. Hard-core woolly worm experts figure the weather accordingly, band by band and week by week. They are such an important part of mountain folklore that the town of Banner Elk, North Carolina, holds an annual Woolly Worm Festival each October. The festival chooses a best in show. The festival features vendors, juried artists, rides, live music, and a woolly worm race. There are similar festivals in Kentucky and Pennsylvania.

Persimmons are rich and delicious fruits that seem to ripen all at once in the fall. They are used in cakes and puddings, and the seeds are cut open to reveal the weather for the coming winter. The kernel inside the body of the seed reveals itself in one of three ways. If it looks like a straight line, it predicts a harsh wind that will cut like a knife. If the kernel resembles a line with a cluster of smaller lines at one end, it is called a "fork" and foretells a mild winter. A line with a small blob at one end is referred to as a "spoon" or "shovel." You'd be right to imagine that means a year with a lot of snow to shovel.

There are other sights and sounds that draw our attention to weather changes. When there is a rainbowlike ring around the moon, it foretells a change in weather—cold rain or even snow within three days. When leaves turn upside down—especially the leaves of poplar and maple trees—it means rain is coming. If the mountain laurel leaves are curled tight, the temperature is below 35 degrees Fahrenheit. Honeybees won't leave their cozy hive-home if the temperature is below 50 degrees. As the twilight temperatures fall in the autumn, you may hear the cheerful buzz of jarflies (a regional name for cicadas). Once you hear a jarfly, it's about six weeks until the first frost. Writing spiders (*Argiope aurantia*) are everywhere in the fall. They are large and handsome and weave zigzags into their webs. Folklore has it that if a writing spider writes your name into her web, you're a goner. But you have to tell her your name first, so you can avoid that particular doom by keeping your mouth shut and not going around introducing yourself to big yellow spiders.

Simple Signs and Omens

What we're discussing here are rightly called *signs and omens*, and people throughout the region have the ability to read both. Signs and omens are two different things though they are often lumped together. A sign is a natural and observed occurrence that gives the observer insight into current and future events. We've just looked at several of those, from woolly worms to persimmon seeds. An omen is usually predictive of something dire and dangerous, a warning of a future event. An omen is something naturally occurring and observed, but unusual and noteworthy. The spider writing your name in her web is an omen. Curling maple leaves are a sign. A wild bird flying into your home is an omen—another death one. When oak leaves are the size of a squirrel's ear, it is a sign that it's time to plant the corn.

It is common in many cultures to ask for a sign when an important decision needs to be made. Most folks will pray over it and wait to be told, which is another version of asking for a sign. Sometimes all we want is a yes or a no. When people use a pendulum, the technique is similar and it is not a subtle art. When you are asking for a sign, you may choose to be specific. If you know the land around you and the creatures that inhabit it with you, you can decide for yourself what sign constitutes an affirmative answer to your question and what sign constitutes a negative one. Here in North Carolina the official state bird is the cardinal, which is easy to spot. Say I'm looking for a sign about whether I should take a job that has been offered to me. There are pros and cons to both options. The job is equally tempting and concerning and I can't quite decide. So I ask the powers that be for a sign. If the answer is yes, I will see a crow. If the answer is no, I'll see a cardinal, effectively showing me the color of a stop sign. Then I wait for my sign. I may also give the powers a deadline, like three days. Or simply whichever one I see first.

The funny thing is that by asking for a sign, the answer to your question usually becomes clear as you wait for the sign. Most people I have talked to keep puzzling it out and sometimes—when that black bird shows up first—they've already decided which sign they want to see. Whether it is an answer from above or the currency to buy a little more thinking time, it can be a helpful trick for making a decision.

There are so many homely signs that are read daily, as casually as you would wipe off the kitchen counter. You have only to mention that your hand itches and the omen is read: right hand itches means you will soon meet a stranger. If your left hand itches, you will get some money. If your nose itches, someone is coming to visit. If your feet itch, you will walk on new land and see sights you haven't seen before. The announcement of an impending visit is always pleasant to consider, especially in the centuries of bad roads and general isolation. If a knife is dropped on the floor, a man will visit. If a spoon, your guest will be a woman. A fork falling to the floor meant a visit from a family.

The best way to discover what was useful and used in your family begins with you listening to those old family stories and then talking to your older relatives. Best if you don't use words like *witch* or *magic*, but ask about those old superstitions that people used to believe. You can also ask for more details in those familiar stories and see what else is remembered of those oft-repeated family myths.

It isn't traditional, but I live by a maxim I call "one, two, three, brick wall," and it has saved me some anxiety over the years. I offer it here for you to consider in your own work. When faced with a problem, I'll think about the possibilities and then will do the simplest thing, which mostly works. But if it doesn't, I kick it up a notch and check the moon phase and sign and try again. If that is still ineffective, I'll pull out all the stops: sun, moon, what's retrograde, herbs, a fancy robe, and a bunch of candles. I'll give it everything I've got. Now if that doesn't work, if I hit a brick wall with my hard head, I know that whatever it is simply isn't my job to do. You see, we often want to help a person or fix a situation in whatever way we can. But sometimes an event occurs or a person is in crisis and they really need to work through it or learn a valuable life lesson. No magical system is foolproof, and no magic worker perfectly adept at all times in all ways. It's good for us to know that we are not the most powerful force in the universe. It keeps us appropriately humble and allows us to try again.

Working with the Moon

By inclination and experience, I am a farmer, a gardener. When I'm touring around teaching and speaking, the soils of these places I wander are of great interest to me. Is it dark and loamy? Sandy? Heavy clay? The native soil here tends to be thin except along river bottom land. It must be heavily amended and built up to make most crops possible. The steep slopes were cleared for crops and the angle of the hills made it difficult to keep the soil in place.

Throughout the mountains, there are stacked stone walls, and the old-timers say that the white settlers made them for two obvious reasons: to remove the stones before and as they plowed the land and to prevent some of the inevitable erosion. These sturdy walls often mark the location of an old homestead, when the house itself is long gone and even the chimney has fallen to rubble.

The garden of my childhood was a sloping piece of good land, situated uphill from the small orchard. I still dream of the homeplace, as I hear many people do. The garden was at the northwest end of the property and the sun was good. There was a freshwater creek that ran down one side and a fold in the ground on the opposite side that we were forbidden to enter. Evidently, my father and some of his friends had decided years before to dynamite the little ravine in search of water. It hadn't worked—and the details were somewhat shady, including the exact location where the charge had been laid. Somehow the dynamite, caps and all, had simply been left where they were. This was something of a theme in my family, this leaving things undone. Most didn't include dynamite, however, and I suspect alcohol was involved.

Daddy called it the Ballard Rock Farm because we could never get all the stones removed from that pretty garden spot. Every year, either when the garden was plowed or when it was harrowed, we hauled rocks from the field to the outside edges of the planting area.

We love to attribute unusual things to "ancient" cultures, but much that we find in the landscape (and in thrift and antique stores) belongs only as far back as our grandparents' generation. These constructed stone walls have the same ancient feel, but a chat with longtime landowners or tenants usually reveals something closer to the present but just as fascinating.

We would all benefit from a better connection to our native soils, no matter what they are. And paying attention to what is over our heads—the moon and the constellations—holds an important place in the folklore of the area too.

It seems that social media has a little hissy fit every time there's a full moon. Heaven forbid there are two in the same calendar month. We have had supermoons and Blood Moons and every month someone posts all the "Native American" names for that particular moon. Those are sometimes self-explanatory, like the Cold Moon of December and the Buck Moon in July. Others are more mysterious but are tied to a landmark occurrence in the natural world, one we may have forgotten or never knew, like the Pink Moon of April and November's Beaver Moon.

It is well-known that farmers and gardeners use the phase and sign of the moon to determine when to do any number of chores. A simple version to remember is that above-ground crops are planted as the moon is waxing to full—in the "light" of the moon. Above-ground crops are the plants that produce their fruit on the branches above the level of the soil. Below-ground crops—like potatoes, carrots, and turnips—are planted in the "dark" of the moon or in the time when the moon is waning to dark and new.

But people do all sorts of things by the phase of the moon, not only planting. You would check on the signs when cutting hair and laying shingles, for brewing, and for starting a diet. Almost every aspect of country life began with a consultation about where the signs were in order to determine exactly when a task should be done. When I was growing up, my dad was pretty simple in his moon following. He followed the rules written above about the light and dark of the moon and that was about it. It seemed to work and it works for me.

Let's break it down. The moon phase is where the moon is in its cycle. The sign is the astrological sign, because it was believed that different astrological signs ruled different parts of the human body. Here's the traditional breakdown:

Aries: Head
Taurus: Neck
Gemini: Arms
Cancer: Chest
Leo: Heart
Virgo: Stomach
Libra: Bowels (called "reins")
Scorpio: Groin (called "secrets")
Sagittarius: Thighs
Capricorn: Knees
Aquarius: Legs
Pisces: Feet

There is an old woodcut-style print called the Man of the Signs that illustrates this. It can be found in any good almanac.

All of this palaver about the moon and the signs also plays an important role in folk healing and folk magic. It can be reduced to "blessing in the light of the moon" and "banes in the dark of the moon." But we are going to unpack that with a bit more intention.

The light of the moon is the time between new moon and full moon. In addition to planting above-ground crops, this energy is good for setting intentions, for blessing babies and newlywed couples. If you consider the workings of an old-fashioned windup pocket watch, this is the energy of the unwinding. Outgoing, vibrant, assertive.

The dark of the moon is the time between full moon and new moon. It's a good time to plant those onions, and the energy is also good for setting boundaries and putting a stop to things that need to be stopped, the activity I refer to as banework. Returning to the image of that dented pocket watch, this is the energy of winding up and going inward. Tightening, receptive.

There is a difference of opinion about the concept of dark moon. When I was coming up, we were taught that dark moon occurs on the nights immediately preceding the appearance of the new moon in the sky. I know some people who consider dark moon and new moon to be the same, but that is not my practice. I use dark moon for the work of extreme healings, the strongest baneworks. It is the lunar time-out-of-time and is the pocket watch neither wound nor unwound.

Some Witchery: Unseen Residents

This is a basic house cleansing with added attention paid to any unseen residents. I ask the homeowner to open all doors and windows, if possible. I leave an offering outside for the land spirits and then spend a few minutes of quiet time, explaining to any resident

spirit folk that it is time for her to go on home to her family. If I
know her name, I address her by name. I usually do this silently
and finish by announcing aloud, "Time to do the house."

I walk through the house, starting at the front door. I carry a
pot of sweet smoke, using my open hand to waft it into all the corners. I do every room—front to back, basement to attic. This can
take a while if it's a big house, so leave yourself plenty of time to do
a thorough job.

I pass through the house a second time, this time ringing a
large bell. I used to use my great-grandmother's dinner bell, but
I bought a small cowbell a few years ago and that sets up a racket,
which is a good thing. Often I'll ask the owners to step outside
because the effects of the ringing can be unpleasant. In fact, if you
do this very often, you may want to use ear protection yourself. I
keep little green ear plugs in my little black bag.

I do a third and final pass through in which I dab a drop of oil
on the door jams, windowsills, fireplace, sinks—all the openings
into (and out of) the house that I can reach. I do this one slowly
too, and I begin again at the front door by placing my hand on the
side of the open door and saying firmly, "Bless this house and all
who enter here."

When I have finished all the dressing-and-blessing work, I
go to stand at the back door and wish the departing spirit a loving farewell and a safe journey home. Let me stress that this can
take a couple of hours to do properly—and you don't want to do a
lick-and-a-promise job here. You can also invite the homeowner to
stand with you for the final farewell part. That can be surprisingly
touching, and involving your client will help them establish their
claim to be the only resident.

Chapter 8

Scraps and Other Useable Pieces

In the bedroom, there is an old chest made by my grandmother that contains a quilt of the sort called a "crazy quilt." It has no discernible pattern but is made up of scraps of fabric, some of them rich and glorious. Real silk, shredded bits of silk velvet, grosgrain, gabardine—the sorts of fabrics that were dear then and are even more rare now. My great-aunt Luna made it, along with several other quilt tops in that same chest. A quilt top, in case you don't know, is the decorative pieced-together layer of a quilt, before it is added to the backing, with batting in between the layers. Then all the layers are pierced through with a threaded needle to hold them together for additional warmth. A handmade quilt is very warm indeed, and many of them—with their stunningly symbolic patterns—are quite beautiful.

These bits and bobs of a family or of a culture serve to hold disparate ideas together and to form a loosely intact piece. So much about my southern Appalachian culture seems unrelated and occasionally unrelatable, but it is held together with the stitches of combined histories of different peoples. It is made manifest in the arts and crafts of the region, in the folk healing and folk magic practices, in the gardens full of healing herbs and hard-won crops. This chapter honors all those beautiful pieces that I can't bring myself to call scraps, though that's exactly what they are. Some are leftovers of migrations, some are remembrances of days past, a few are revenants of bigger pieces lost in the integration of cultures or families.

Experiencing the presence of disembodied spirits—the sort considered in the witchery at the end of the previous chapter— is another possible legacy from those much-maligned forebears. There are ghost-hunting shows all over cable TV and ghost tours in larger cities. So many people long to experience a ghost but few do. If this is a skill you have gotten, you know it isn't always fun or even interesting. It is a doorway that can be difficult to close once it is opened.

Here in the southern highlands of the old Appalachian Mountains, we pondered the unusual autumn season last year. Generally speaking, the sassafras turns its haunting red earlier than the rest, followed by the yellow glow of maples, then all the rest: an unbelievably beautiful finale for the end of the summer. In western North Carolina, it is safe to count on peak color the third weekend in October, sooner in the higher elevations like Mt. Mitchell and Blowing Rock. Peak weekend came and went and the old hills were still mostly green.

Was it a sign of global climate confusion? Late season rains from a couple of hurricanes that devastated the coast? An omen about the consequences of being too lightly connected to the landscape that is home, as well as pantry?

The omen readers delivered some wary thoughts and we common folk simply waited, appreciating the contrast of the occasional splash of scarlet against the still-green deciduous trees.

Our ancestors had to know what was going on with the weather and the changing seasons because their lives and their livelihoods depended on that knowledge. They noted shifting wind patterns and knew what the changes would entail and how those changes would impact where they were in the agricultural cycle.

They started from the ground up—and from the clouds down.

Permaculture teaches that it is best to tend the soil and the plants growing in it will tend themselves. Healthy, microbe-rich soil with a vibrant collection of earthworms produces healthy plants. Thick mulch and the requisite levels of water and sunshine provide everything a plant needs to be productive.

From the ground up.

Soil suddenly feels like a metaphor for human communities as well. A vibrant and healthy community grows in the good soil of mutual respect, engaged listening and kindness, with a dash of good humor.

Following the example of our ancestors, coming into a deep relationship with the land on which we live benefits our human community in many ways. And when we take responsibility for whatever part we play in the continuing degradation of the natural world, the land benefits from our good and consistent attention. Symbiotic relationships benefit all parties, which is a happy change from the dominion language of Genesis that seems to impact much of our engagement with the earth.

Before our species developed agriculture, we were nomadic, gathering our sustenance through hunting and gathering. Roots, nuts, and berries for food and leaves and mosses for food and medicine. We found allies all along the way, in all sorts of climates, in all kinds of landscapes. When we started to settle down and settle in, we also started saving seed and taming animals for meat, eggs, fiber.

Our relationship to the green world shifted then as it would continue to do throughout our history. These changes were magnified when certain major religious movements pulled us away from our animist views and recentered the sacred away from the land. Since that time, as a species, we have come to think ourselves superior to the natural world, removed from it, no longer beholden to it.

This is an old story, one that still clings to much of our public policy in the United States and to some adherents of those same religions that convinced many of our ancestors that their best shot for a better life wasn't earthly but heavenly, only accessible after death, but then it would be glorious. But not now and not here. Not in this sordid and sinful world.

I look out the front window into the dark yard where the shapes of shrubs and medicinal herbs shimmy in a light early winter breeze. The sturdy witch hazel, which can't decide if it's a large bush or a small tree, spreads its flat and golden leaves over the walkway and the squatting rhododendron. It will hold on to those leaves long after they have gone from gold to brown to gray, only abandoning their post when the blooms come in late December. The maples next door loom above the herb bed and the witch hazel. Those leaves are long gone, raked up, and poured onto the compost pile, destined to be soil in a couple of years.

Humans tend to anthropomorphize the natural world, making it smaller, less frightening, and controllable. I imagine that the witch hazel that I planted so long ago is "shimmying." Their shapes in the street-lighted city darkness loom like friendly creatures—camels and cows and giraffes. But they are none of those things. They are the result of millions of years of evolution and will do whatever they can to survive, even as the planet warms and the storms become stronger. They adapt where and as they can, but sometimes they can't adapt fast enough. Those plants are chosen for extinction and we find them embedded now in stones, find them petrified still holding the shapes that couldn't adapt quickly enough.

The city I live in is a Tree City. That doesn't save any of our trees from the developers that want to clear the land they've purchased and build something large and profitable on it. But we have signs at the city limits to remind visitors that we love trees. As a town, we pretend we have a relationship to these elder kindred that we don't, in fact, honor.

And that also cycles my thoughts back to the Pagan community, which isn't far from my mind most days. We often lay claim to a deeper connection to the planet than non-Pagans, as we honor the cardinal directions and the classical elements. We are happy to tell you about our holidays, pointing out the solstices and equinoxes, and the cross-quarter days that lie between, harkening back to the cycle of a northern European agricultural year.

We may follow that cycle through ritual and ceremony, but for many of us it has become merely symbolic, the connection thinned out or broken. Those of us who are urban dwellers blame our surroundings—not enough green, parks, street trees. We stay inside when we are home from work and we read books and meet our cyber communities through screens. We dream of intentional communities that we will create someday. Earthen or green building, fields of organic vegetables, chickens with artisanal chicken tractors, and neighbors who follow the same basic spirituality as we do—what could be better? And we continue to live in apartments and condos and once a year we attend our favorite summer festival where we dance awkwardly around bonfires and dream our dreams.

But there is no reason we can't pursue a relationship with the world around us whether we live in a suburb or inner city, in an apartment or dorm. We can make it real, the landscape around us. We can enter into the enchantment that lies under concrete, that flows from one block to the next through the crosswalk. When we set out to fall in love with our landscape, no matter what that landscape is or where, we touch that deep mystery, that enchantment that we dream of at Pagan festivals.

We talked about those betwixt places—hedgerows and other liminal places—in an earlier chapter, but it may be wise here to renew our acquaintance with the possibilities of these places that are neither here nor there. The truth is that these old mountains, with their folds, hollers, and old trails, with their mica mines and forgotten amusement parks, have a strangeness to them that most visitors can sense right away. It isn't simply the folktales that accrue to places like Judaculla Rock and Linville Gorge. It is the sense of the mountains themselves with their history of migrants and the interaction of the residents to the unseen beings that so many mountain people acknowledge, even when they don't want to.

There are places hidden in the landscape, hikers lost in the laurels, visitors who wander too close to the edge of a waterfall and end up at the bottom.

Tea as Metaphor ... and Drink

One of my delights is to sit with friends over a cup of tea, or as I call it, a cuppa. Whether we consider it a medicinal miracle, a warming beverage, or a social requirement, sitting down to a cup of tea is a ritual that needs to be reactivated in our coffee-guzzling culture. The Japanese and Chinese have the right idea—make a ritual out of this simple act of hospitality and you change the world and yourself in it.

You can use tea bags or tea balls. The point is the infusion of water with a specific herb. Few things are as warming on a cold, damp day than a hot cup of tea. Black and green tea are made from the tea plant, *Camellia sinensis*, which is native to East Asia but is now grown in many places throughout the world. But any edible herb, flower, fruit, or seed can be steeped in hot or boiling water and drunk as a tea. The beverage may be sweetened with whatever suits you and whitened with whatever milk or cream you prefer. The leaves can be used for divination, as we discussed earlier. Any kind of tea may be served hot or cold, and the South is well-known for its love of sweet iced tea.

A Nice Cuppa

There is much to be said for the homely power of a simple cup of tea or coffee. Mountain folks would often keep a pot of coffee on the stove and drink it all day long. Coffee is often served black as night and strong as death, but if you ask nicely, there might be a drop of fresh milk or cream to lighten it up for you. Hospitality is a sacred duty in many cultures and mine is no exception. When you are invited onto the porch or into the kitchen, that is a sign of respect and sometimes affection. Many modern practitioners replace that strong coffee with beautifully medicinal herbs.

A cup of tea is healing for body and soul. When you have no idea what to say when a friend is confronted with loss and trag-edy, a proffered cup of tea and a quiet gathering at your kitchen table may begin her healing process. A cup of good black tea in the middle of your busy afternoon is a chance to refocus, to retool, and to relax. So many of us race through life, chasing our tales for our boss or our families. Be still for a bit and hold a warm cup of your favorite tea. Spend time with yourself and remember what you really want and who you really are. A different sort of magic and not confined to my beloved culture, but it is a magic accessible to everyone and only requires the simplest ingredients and a little bit of technique. And time, something that is incredibly precious, even if we don't always realize that.

Asheville had a St. Patrick's Day Festival for a few years but soon found that mid-March is not a good time for an outdoor festival here. The week before the vernal equinox is often cold and rainy and those few years were no exception. Our theater company was performing and we had an info booth too, as I recall. The rain and cold started to seep into my bones, but there were hours to go before we could go home. There was a vendor who was offering Scottish food—mostly scones and soda bread—and I wandered over to warm up my feet. The lady there was dressed for the weather and remarkably cheerful.

Salves and Poultices

Poultices and salves are traditional in Appalachian culture. Poultices are grated or chopped material (onions, potatoes, herbs) that is wrapped in cotton muslin and applied directly to the skin. Onion and mustard poultices were used on the chest when someone had a bad cold. It was believed to draw out the sickness. My best experience of this technique was on my father's feet. He came back from North Africa and World War II with a fungal infection on his feet. As a result, his feet got hot easily and were flaky and itchy. It was something that tormented him the whole time I was growing up. I don't remember who told me about grated potatoes for skin ailments, but we tried it soon after. It took several weeks of occasional application but the treatment finally worked, and he was only bothered in the hottest part of the summer after that. The potato poultice turned black with exposure to air (and to my dad's feet), and when it started to dry out, my dad washed it off his feet.

A salve is a pomade that is applied directly to the skin for the treatment of various ills. Salves are often made with beeswax and some kind of oil as a base that is heated gently, and herbs are added to the soft mixture. The salve is then poured into containers, where it firms up as the mixture cools. A black salve (also called drawing salve) is used for splinters, boils, and the like because it pulls the corruption from the body. The active ingredients in a drawing salve are usually plantain oil, kaolin clay, and charcoal powder. I use an over-the-counter arnica salve for skin tags and dry patches. Many modern salves use petroleum jelly as their base, but that isn't traditional.

Tinctures and Oils

I make lots of tinctures and oils. I tincture most everything in alcohol, drinking alcohol. I used to use the cheapest vodka on the bottom shelf of my local Alcoholic Beverage Control store, but I gave away more and more of that stuff in the winter and people began complaining that it tasted harsh and was hard to swallow with a sore throat. I switched to rum or gin after that, and the taste of some of the tinctures improved immensely.

Making tincture is about the closest most of us come to old-time alchemy. Here's how I do it (which I just found out is called "the folk method"):

Any size glass jar will do, as long as it has a well-sealing lid. I almost always use plain old canning (Mason) jars with a fresh lid. Give the jar a thorough cleaning with hot water and dish soap, even if it's brand new. Dry it with a clean towel. I don't sterilize these jars, like the ones I use when canning, because the alcohol in the tincture takes care of that for me.

The plant parts to use will depend on the tincture you are making, so you'll have to check your recipe to see if it is roots, leaves, stems, berries, flowers, or a combination. There will be many variations for the recipe but the technique is common.

Fill your clean jar with the plant material, about two-thirds to three-quarters full. If they are berries, put your clean fist into the jar and mash them up good. Fill the jar with a high-octane drinkable alcohol, because you will be ingesting this tincture and minimizing the powerful taste—especially of some roots—will make that tasting a more pleasant experience. I use 80-proof clear alcohol or higher, if I can get it. Traditional Appalachian medicines tend to use the native alcohol, which is high proof and also illegal. I use rum, vodka, and sometimes gin, depending on the plant materials. Some folks like to use brandy, which is very tasty, or Everclear, which is very strong. Cover the jar tightly and leave in a dark place for a moon cycle, shaking once a day. After the month is up, strain the liquid off and store in a cool place.

Receipts

Receipt is an old-fashioned word for *recipe* and is the word that some Appalachian cove doctors used to refer to a written-out spell (because they didn't use the word *spell*) or for a written-out list of ingredients and instructions for making a particular tasty dish, the definition we are more accustomed to seeing. In those vintage cookbooks—like *The Wise Encyclopedia of Cookery*—that can be found in any used book store, a smart person will check out the formerly blank pages in the back. Cookbook publishers often left several blank pages in cookbooks so the thrifty housewife could pencil in her favorite new recipes. These recipes might include a neighbor's special spice cake recipe, or the best way to slaughter and dress a groundhog, or a few lines of prayer to be said for a birthing mother. If you inherited old cookery books from family members, be sure to check out those back pages and see if you can read the spidery handwriting.

Many modern Appalachian folks, as well as far-flung members of the Appalachian diaspora, are curious whether members of their own family were yarb doctors or granny healers. It is wise to refrain from asking about "witches" in the family or whether anyone practiced magic. That language will usually shut a conversation down and close off those avenues of information. Best to ask about those old superstitions that folks held to or inquire if there were members of the family who were known as healers or who were midwives. You can also talk about things you've read about and wonder aloud if things like prophetic dreams are a real thing. You may be surprised at what you learn about the people in your own family, because most hillfolks are natural storytellers—one of the stereotypes about us that happens to be true.

Sachets

While we're on the subject of language and what we call things here—which is sometimes similar to what you may have heard and sometimes very different—let's go over a couple more interesting bits of mountain folk healing and magic. The word *sachet* is used for a folded paper spell and also for a protective bag, like a mojo bag, that hangs around your neck. It is pronounced with the final T: *saa-shett*, with the emphasis on the first syllable. Let's look at both possibilities.

A folded piece of paper might hold some dried herbs, a shiny dime, some red thread, and something sharp, like a small thorn or bit of broken glass. This is a protection charm and would be carried in the pocket of an apron or a pair of work pants. There are also folded paper charms for removing all sorts of ailments, from toothache to gout.

A sachet might also refer to a small cotton bag worn on a string around the neck. This might contain similar goods as in a pocket sachet—something sharp, something reflective, needful herbs, and the like. It might also contain a little chunk of asfidity. Asafoetida is its real name, and it is a resin from a plant in the same genus as fennel (*Ferula*) and is used in some Indian cooking. It has a powerfully pungent smell, somewhere in the area of rotting garlic, stinky onions, and warm ramps, and was believed to repel all sorts of diseases as well as wandering and harmful spirit folks. It was very popular during the influenza pandemic of 1918, when twenty to fifty million people died, almost a million in the US.

In one of our family burial plots, there's a chipped marker for my great-uncle's first wife. As everything seems to be in the southern highlands of Appalachia, a visit to the family plot brought a cautionary tale. This woman was pregnant in 1918 and contracted the H1N1 influenza virus, the one that caused that pandemic and is still around today. I can still hear my grandmother's voice: "If a pregnant woman got that flu, it was a death sentence." When I do the math, my grandmother was fourteen years old in 1918. It must have had a profound effect on her, her sister-in-law's death. And I wonder whether she tended the sickbed, as she did with her husband when he died of tuberculosis decades later.

Asfidity is best known now as a spice, but its folkloric use as a disease preventative was once quite common. A small clump of it was worn in a sachet around the neck, as described above. In addition to its use against disease, it was also believed to keep bad spirits from attaching to you. When you consider how little we knew about viruses and bacteria, it makes sense that unseen things that could attack you might be seen in the same light.

I have a big chunk of asfidity that friends ordered for me as a joke, I suspect. It is very hard and must be cracked with a hammer, like a black walnut. I have an asfidity dressing/anointing oil tincturing on my workbench. I want to find new uses for this powerful herb.

It is kept in a ziplock bag, inside another plastic bag, inside a canning jar, inside another heavy plastic bag. The smell permeates the travel case it resides in. If I'm teaching on a hot day and the travel case stays in the car for any length of time, there will be a faint but unmistakable odor that permeates the interior of the car for days after.

Herbalists, as you know by now, are a hardy and eccentric breed. I was teaching at an organic growers conference a couple of years ago and asfidity was part of the class on folk healing. I stopped by the information table to speak to some friends and mentioned I had it with me. One of my friends excitedly asked to see it—by which she meant "smell it" because it isn't much to look at, to be honest—and I opened up the travel bag and handed her the heavily muffled rock. A group started to gather as she laid aside plastic bags, unscrewed the top of the canning jar, stuck her nose in the jar and inhaled deeply. Then she passed it to the next person who did the same. This repeated several more times as they discussed uses for it, and I explored the folkways I knew that surrounded its use. After it was rewrapped and stored away, the pungent smell lingered in the air at that info table. As it tends to do. It is one of those smells that comes in through your nose and hits the back of your soft palate so that you also taste it.

Asfidity is a known abortifacient and an emmenagogue (an herb that increases the flow of menstrual blood), so be very careful handling it and do not ingest it at all, except in the minute amounts found in delicious Indian food. Got it?

Dollies and Poppets

Most cultures also have a tradition of poppets, dolls made of many different materials that are stand-ins for humans. We are probably most familiar with "voodoo dolls," but the miniature ivory female figures, called medicine or diagnostic dolls, that were used in Imperial China by male doctors to examine their female patients are also poppets.

We call them dollies or doll-babies. They are sometimes exactly that—a lovingly crafted but primitive child's toy. You've seen the wizened apple-faced dolls and the ones made of rags or corn shucks. Sometimes a face is carved into a knob of wood or a fat stick and given to a child to dress with whatever scraps were available in mother's workbasket or with leaves and flowers from the yard and garden. We used to take those wide tulip poplar leaves and pinch off the stem. We'd fold it into a hat and pierce the leaf with the stem to hold that cap shape. They were always too small for our heads and usually ended up on a doll or a cat.

Dollies are used for any number of things. A person-shaped scrawl on a piece of paper might have words written on it, and these could be prayers for healing, charms for pregnancy, or love spells for enticing someone. They could contain baneful words to bring the targeted person down in the world or to otherwise harm them. The paper was then burned, buried, or thrown into the outhouse hole.

Poppetry is an exquisite and subtle art, and poppets are best made of materials with which the maker is familiar and has some skill in manipulating. Such a simple, homely thing—we often overlook the effectiveness of a dolly utilized by someone with the ability to put it to its best use. Certainly, you can buy an adorable little keychain at a shop that has a note identifying it as your boss or mother-in-law or ex. This appropriation of a legitimate and ancient cultural artifact is very popular but of limited value, except as a way to find your keys in the bottom of your purse. TV and film have given us all sorts of images of dolls stuck with pins and the immediate result of the hero character. A jab to the chest and the person in whose image the doll was made clutches his chest. A jab to the leg and he falls over. The person holding the poppet is furious but gleeful with every jab.

Wax is very good for poppets, easily malleable. In lieu of that, modeling or polymer clays are colorful and equally easy to use. There is something very old-school about using beeswax, especially if it comes from your own bees. It smells nice, for one thing, and, because you have a relationship with the beings that made the stuff, you know what has gone into its creations. Bees have to ingest eight ounces of honey to create one ounce of beeswax. It is labor intensive for them, which makes the material especially potent. Dollies can also be carved from materials like wood and soap.

Corn shucks are readily available in places where corn is food for animal and human, where it's ground to meal, or where the stalks are burned for warmth. Fresh shucks are easily manipulated into a doll shape and can be tied with thin strips of the same material, and dried shucks are easily reconstituted in a pan of water or a creek.

All these quilt scraps and this garden medicine are part and parcel of the hill ways that we are reviving and continuing and, in some cases, reinventing. I am not the only one, of course. Nobody owns these ways because, well, we all do. It is our birthright as sure as inheriting the family homeplace. Some of us have set it aside, and some of us are ashamed of these primitive, simple roots that sustain us. A vast Appalachian diaspora is filled with people who dream of a home here that they never truly knew, and they are a part of this story too.

Some Witchery:
Ways to Stop Gossip and Backbiting
A Taste of Your Own Medicine
This working is effective for gossip, rudeness, plain old hateful behavior. Fill a small bottle with vinegar or lemon juice. Place three black peppercorns in it and add a tiny metal nail or brad. Write the person's name on a slip of paper and roll it up, as you roll up a dolly, and place it into the bottle. Put a cork in or the lid on the bottle and seal it closed with wax. Throw it into rapidly running water (a river or large creek) or bury it off your property.

Hush Your Mouth
Alum is a handy ingredient for puckering up the mouth and putting an end to gossip. Take a small jar, put a piece of alum in it (or a pinch of alum powder) and write the name or names of the people who are destroying your reputation. Leave it in a place that is secret and protected and let it work its magic for a moon cycle.

A classic one that isn't at all traditional is piercing a beef tongue with nails or long thorns and freezing it to "freeze the tongue" of the gossiper.

Chapter 9

Hillfolk Gothic: Haints and Haint Tales

To be an Appalachian native is to wake in the cool mist of a spring morning and listen to birds in their daybreak ruckus. It is an invitation to sit on a neighbor's porch and listen to a ballad singer or musician, and to hear stories of near-mythic relatives who did this, that, and frequently the other. If you spend your life in an urban setting, where your native accent can hinder your career, you may feel like you've unbuttoned your trousers after a big meal when you can once again talk among people who sound like you.

But there is a whiff of twilight in this old culture, a sense of dusk but rarely dawn. I have come to refer to this state of delighted endarkenment as Hillfolk Gothic. It isn't the familiar Southern Gothic of steamy nights and moss-draped oaks. It is a thing less genteel, more ragged and less urban, older, and less malevolent than uncaring. We humans have been here for so little time in these strange old mountains. Our oddness barely makes a dent in the shreds of spirit and memory that linger here.

The three main things that make up Hillfolk Gothic are witchery, the elusive beings we call "boogers" (a group that includes the Fair Folk and land spirits), and hauntings.

We'll end the chapter and the book with some ghost tales. But there are also spirit folks that aren't exactly people and you need to know a little about them too. We don't know if the earliest people here had traditions of spirit beings who were mostly invisible but chose to interact with humans. We do know the Cherokee have tales about the moon-eyed people as well as the Nunnehi, who are spirit people. And each set of immigrants brought their own stories of spirit beings.

There are stories of cryptids here—Sasquatch and dog-men—who are sometimes identified in grainy photographs but more often seen out of the corner of the eye. There are true believers with tales of their own, but I have never experienced these strange others.

The ones I know best (who help me in my garden and in my work) are the land spirits that I call the Cousins. I describe them as a herd of invisible miniature dachshunds, but the truth is I sense them more than see them. Their presence brings a sparkling to the air around them, a mist of champagne bubbles. We learned years ago that they are friendly and mostly kind when they are given respect and offered hospitality. They like to be given strong coffee and terrible candy—the sort of food coloring– and sugar-laden stuff that little kids love and adults only eat as a guilty pleasure. Shaped like worms or fish or hamburgers, dusted with sour sugar, and dyed in colors not found in nature, these offerings are such a delight to them, I suspect, because the candies aren't part of their world. Same with the coffee we offer. They also like bright shards of broken glass and those flat-bottomed glass beads used in some floral arrangements. Leave these gifts in your garden or in a pretty bowl on your kitchen table.

In some homes, the kitchen window holds a chipped (and therefore unusable) canning jar with bits of broken colorful glass, a sort of homespun stained glass. I can remember three such decorations in the kitchens of my childhood. The mother or grandmother kept adding pretties until the jar was full. If asked about it, they would exclaim that the children's bare feet had to be protected, and, besides, isn't it so bright and cheering? This is a talisman that came from Britain and is designed to keep baneful spirits from entering the heart of the house. Mischievous spirits are always drawn to the warmth of fellowship of the kitchen, and they could be kept from their mischief in the house by means of that simple jar charm. You see, those little stinkers can't pass up a jar full of edges—they must count each and every edge, but they are not good at counting and also have dim memories. So it keeps them there on the sill until they tire of the game and leave the kitchen (and the rest of the house) unmolested. They stay stuck in the window and never get inside to sour the milk and cause the biscuits to burn.

I have no explanation for the other sort of being I've encountered, so I will simply relate what I know. I was sitting with a friend on the front porch of their old frame house when a summer storm came roaring up the holler and over the hill. The night had been hot and humid, as mountain nights can sometimes be in the height of summer, and the storm came on fast, the clouds lowering onto the hilltops. Flash and rumble almost at once and in rapid succession. It was glorious. As the light show lessened and the rain came on, we watched the ridgeline. There was something there, something moving. Several inconclusive shadows moved slowly along the ridge, taller than the trees there and shaped like a drop of water. But solid looking. I don't know who or what they are, but I suspect they are somehow the very spirit of these old mountains and, like them, will endure.

We hold a special sense of respect for the kith and kindred who have made the transition from matter to spirit—the ghosts that seem to be around every corner.

Ours is a land haunted by its history, and that is obvious in the haunted houses, barns, churches, and covered bridges that litter the landscape. My daughter has had the gift of communicating with spirit folk since she was in middle school. My mother had it too, the gift seeming to skip a generation. We were always chasing after local ghosts, and if she were alive today, she'd be one of those paranormal investigators with beeping equipment and night-vision goggles.

It comes and goes with me. I get called out several times a year to help a frightened homeowner or renter figure out what's going on. Mostly we don't know the story—we experience the imprint of a life. There was a girl in a blue dress, sitting in the hayloft of a friend's barn. There's the sad old woman who returned to the house where she raised her children—my little farmhouse—after she died in a local nursing home. There was the host of shining beings descending an invisible staircase as a fiddler played a solemn air.

Calling the Dead

Setting aside the silly notion of "Necro Wafers," there may be times in life when you are looking to call the dead to you. You may choose to do this as part of your work in ancestor veneration and invite your people in when you set up their offerings. For several years now, I've left food at the cemetery that is the final resting place of many of the people I've written about in this book. I developed a spirit-drawing water that I spray on their headstones by using a pump bottle. The water is equal parts corn liquor, spring water, apple juice (from my own apples), and coffee essence. I spray the water first, then set out the food and other offerings I've brought for my people. Then I welcome them in.

If your people are buried in a public place, please be careful not to leave litter at the graves. Food disappears quickly, so leave it on the ground, no plates or cups. If you're nervous about it, you can talk to the office personnel and explain that it is a "family tradition." It may be best to quietly leave your offerings and not draw attention to it. The alternative, of course, is to offer these things on an outdoor ancestor altar in your own backyard. The spray will help with that too.

You may choose to directly engage with the dead in order to get information, including whether a recently deceased loved one is doing well in the afterlife. This may include asking for and then looking for a sign that all is well. That sign could be the appearance of a particular bird or a talisman that is significant to the one you loved. The spirit who inhabits the house at the little farm is fond of leaving coins all over the place. One of us can sweep and mop the floor and return moments later to find a shiny dime. We keep them in a large jar in the dining room.

You may certainly connect in this way by engaging the services of a reputable psychic medium. Get recommendations from people you trust and schedule a short session before shelling out a bunch of money. There are unscrupulous people who will try to take advantage of your grief to drain your bank account. Be sensible. Ask your question, get your answer, and let that be that.

Your loved ones may choose to contact you through a dream state, either when sleeping or daydreaming. My cousin Evie had seen her husband through several different cancers before brain cancer finally killed him. So many members of the family told her he'd come to them in dreams, but she was sad that he'd never done that for her. Almost exactly a year later, she dreamed she was sitting on her covered porch, but the scene in front of her was not the neighbors' house but a large cornfield. There was someone working out there and she thought she could make out his familiar silhouette. As she watched, he straightened his back and turned to face her. He waved and then watched her for a moment before returning to his task. She was satisfied by both his appearance and the message.

My mother, as I believe I have mentioned, had an affinity for spirit folk. She also liked mynah birds and introduced me to the works of Asimov, Lovecraft, and Sybil Leek. And yet she refused to think of herself as a witch, which is always a person's right and her choice to make. Still, there were many times when we sat listening to one of her ghost stories, or that time she saw her deceased aunt floating on a cloud. There were also the table tilting and the séances.

No, really. I carry such a distinct memory of a ratty old card table and four of us around the table—my mother, me, probably my cousin Dena, and maybe my brother. It was evening and the lights were low in the house. We concentrated so hard and the table did move a little. I never knew if it was a legitimate encounter or if somebody was fudging the results. We did it several times and we even added a Ouija board. I have never been nervous about spirit boards, either because of those early controlled uses or because they are such sovereign tools. There was all sorts of panic a decade ago when a popular national toy chain offered a pretty pink

Ouija board kit to all those would-be witch girls. Yes, of course I bought one for my daughter. Not that she needed it—she has the knack for that, as we say.

I sometimes lead a ghost tour in downtown Asheville and tell the stories that only the locals know and don't often share. It isn't done in a sensationalized way—merely a simple telling of a story about dead folks who usually don't know that they are. We also do an evening of ghost stories as a fundraiser for our Goddess temple sometimes, and this chapter includes some of the stories that have stuck with me over the years. We'll end our time together here with what everyone likes to glean from an old culture: ghost tales and stories of mystery. We'll piece them together like a good quilt—a square of wonderment sandwiched between two haint tales. I hope it'll keep you warm as the year and the light starts to fade.

Enjoy.

A Haint Tale: The Little Rock House

During the summer, it was hard to keep us away from the little store down across from the gas station. We called it the Penny Candy Store because you could buy some of the candy there for a penny. One of our mothers—who didn't work outside their homestead and didn't drive either—would send the whole bunch of us down the hill to get a pack of cigarettes or saltine crackers. Sometimes I rode down on my pony and wrapped the reins around one of the porch's columns until I came out with a can of Coke in one hand, some candy in the other, and a pack of Winstons tucked in the front bib of my overalls. We'd sit on the bench outside the store like old men around a pickle barrel and we'd eat our preferred candy and drink our off-brand soda and watch the world go by. The pony usually shared the candy but not always.

There was one house that we passed just before we got to the store. We would walk past it on the other side of the narrow paved road and we'd go slowly, so we could keep an eye on it. In a place where all the houses were made of wood, logs, or bricks, this one stood out, for it was covered with river rock. Walls, porch, everywhere. It was wood underneath—or so we were told—but you couldn't see a bit of it, except for the steps going up to the little stoop of a porch.

We walked slowly because we knew the story of that old house. Years before, right after it was built and when it was still wooden, there was a couple living there who did not get along. They'd yell and cuss and fight until the neighbors were weary of the commotion. Each gave as good as they got—him being mean and her being mean and sassy.

It all came to a head one Sunday when the lady was sitting on the porch steps and the fella demanded she go with him to church. "I ain't going to church," she told him.

"You are going to church. Get yourself dressed right now."

"I am not going to church."

That kept on for a while until the fella snapped. "You are going to church one way or the other!" he yelled, as he came out the front door with a big knife from the kitchen. He cut her throat before she could say a word and the blood went everywhere. He dragged her halfway into the house, and she was struggling and he did some more stabbing before he—and she—was finished.

The neighbors got suspicious because it was so quiet over there and finally came over to find her dead halfway between the porch and the linoleumed living room, him crying like a baby in the kitchen and blood everywhere.

She went to church all right, and he went to prison, or so we were told. The blood stains would not come out of the wooden house, and it was decided that it would all be covered with rock from the river so no one would ever be the wiser. But she makes sure no one forgets what happened there because she can still be seen, in the early morning and in the evening as the sun sets, lying on the porch with a dark slash across her throat. And as you go past the house, she turns her head to watch you go, but she can't call out because her throat is cut.

A Haint Tale: The Bride and Groom on Pisgah

I like coming back to good old Mt. Pisgah for this tale. In addition to the Rat that climbs the side of the mountain, there is a phenomenon that only happens after a good snowfall. The light and shadows on the slope of the mountain form what looks like a bride and groom. There's a tallish figure on the one side and a shorter figure at its side that looks like it's wearing a head covering and a long dress. I personally think it looks more like a squirrel but that doesn't make for such a good legend.

The Bride and Groom on Pisgah has been noted for many years. Like most stories, there are variations on a theme about the reason for the phenomenon—so many legends, so many stories— but I'm going to relate the one I've always heard and add some embellishment to make it a tale.

There was a plain girl who lived in a cove on the flanks of Mt. Pisgah. She was smart and strong but she wasn't what you'd call pretty. She was the oldest of a big family of mostly boys and her mama had died when the littlest one was birthed. She knew how to do everything around the house. That gal could sew and cook and bake. She tended the stock and seemed to have such a knack with growing things that she didn't just have a green thumb, she had two green hands. She was her daddy's pride and joy, and he was happy she was so plain because that meant she'd stay in his house forever.

She had a sweet singing voice too, and that was the thing that ended up being the death of her.

This gal, let's call her Margaret, was out in the garden one sunny afternoon. She was singing and pulling a few weeds out of the potato patch. The big 'Mortgage Lifter' tomatoes were filling out and the tommy toes were pinking up.

Now, the family that lived down the cove had had a recent bereavement. The woman of the house had lost her sister and her sister's husband to the influenza down state. The last child of the family was still at home—almost grown but sickly himself from tending both his parents and grieving from his bereavement. So he had gone to live with his aunt and uncle until he was strong enough to go his own way in the world. We'll call him Will.

It was a warm day and Will was venturing out for the first time. He was a little shaky but not doing too bad when he heard a sound that warmed him from his heart all the way up to his face, and he smiled for the first time in months. It was Margaret singing, of course. He followed the sound to the edge of a big kitchen garden and at that moment, Margaret jumped up from her squatting position, let out an angry squeal and grabbed her hoe. As Will watched, she swung it over her head and struck once, twice, three times before stepping back. Will was slowly making his way over to her when she turned and saw him. She was holding up by its tail the copperhead she had just killed with the hoe. She was proud of herself all right. A bite from that ill creature would have caused her some harm.

Will thought she was the most beautiful thing he had ever seen. Strong, smiling, capable.

She walked to him, still holding the headless snake.

"Well, that is something," Will said, by way of introduction. He started to put out his hand but thought better of it. "I'm staying with my aunt and uncle down the road. I'm Will."

She nodded and told her name. That's where it all started. Those two young people threw that snake into the woods and then sat on a log together. After some talking, she showed him the spring, and they both had a cool drink. Then Will took himself home and Margaret went back to the garden.

Every day after that, those two would meet up and talk. Margaret had him help with her chores and Will grew stronger. She would bring out cold cornbread and buttermilk for her dinner and always brought enough for him too. By the time the apples were coming in, he was well enough to climb the trees and shake the best ones down.

When the pumpkin-colored October full moon rose up, the two figured out that they were in love, the real thing. And they decided the next thing to do would be to tell their families and set a date with the preacher.

They decided they'd best tell her daddy first, but he was gone into town to do some trading and wouldn't likely be back for a fortnight. Since they couldn't wait to tell someone, they went down the road to Will's aunt and uncle, who were very happy because even though she was plain, Margaret was all the things you'd want for your young man.

They smooched and held hands—and made apple butter and chow-chow—until Margaret's father finally got home. He had barely settled in when the pair cornered him to ask his permission and celebrate the good news.

Only there wasn't good news because her father was not one bit happy for them. He had set his mind on having her there forever and he refused to allow it. Will was brokenhearted and Margaret was mad as a bandy rooster. She had worked her whole life to make their place run smooth and look smart and this was the thanks she got. Will walked home with his tail between his legs, but Margaret started to plot and scheme.

She gave her father the silent treatment and that just made him more determined. She stopped cooking anything that could be eaten and that made her father madder. Finally, she blurted out, "I am going to marry him, and you can't stop me!"

He locked her in her room, yelling, "I will kill that boy before I'll let him marry you and haul you off!"

After a few days, he let her out and she was even quieter than before. Her silence hung over the house like a funeral pall. She bided her time and she found ways to slip out and meet Will, who was broken-hearted until he heard her plan. The preacher would be down in town for Christmas, and they would sneak away and meet him and get married. They'd run away downstate to where Will had grown up and where he knew folks. All would be well; they only had to be careful.

Three days before Christmas there was snow and a layer of rime ice on everything. Colder than usual and getting about was rough. Most people put their animals in the barns and hayed them down good and stayed indoors themselves.

On Christmas Eve, Margaret put on her best dress, warm clothes on top of that, and a thick shawl over it all. She put on an old wool hat and picked up a little carpetbag with what few things she cherished and she set out into the lowering twilight.

Will met her at the spring, similarly dressed, and they started on the uphill path that would take them away. They were holding hands and dreaming the kind of dreams that make young people feel warmth on a cold night in the mountains.

They had gotten only partway up the steepest part of the path when they heard hound dogs and distant shouts. Her daddy had discovered she was gone and had set the dogs out to find her. The two of them picked up their pace though the rime ice was worse here and they had to be careful.

The dogs and the shouting got closer and closer and finally they could see him. His face was red with his anger, and he was carrying the shotgun. They stopped at the edge of the path, and put their arms around each other, and waited. They were going to have to face the music, it seemed, and so they would.

The dogs loved Margaret, and when they saw her they leaped and drooled and jumped right on her. Her daddy was yelling and threatening all kinds of violence, but when he saw how tenderly Will was holding his sweet girl, his heart softened.

It was about then that the biggest hound caught up with the others and jumped right into the middle of Margaret's chest. His weight and the rime ice combined to throw her backward, and she lost her balance. She fell off the edge of the path and down into the night, taking Will and the hound with her.

Her daddy carefully stepped to the edge and looked down. He could see them far below, still and silent, their limbs in awkward and unnatural positions. Taking his kerosene lantern in one hand and a stout stick in the other, it still took him the good part of an hour—and much sliding and cussing—to get to them. They were both dead and the hound dog sat beside them howling to beat the band.

They were buried side by side in the family graveyard up from her house, and her father never did forgive himself. Every time it snowed throughout his long and mournful life, he could see them there on the side of Pisgah, dressed in their heavy winter clothes and holding hands, their love carved out in snow and rime ice for all the world to see.

A Haint Tale: The Sleeping Man from Opelika

My mother's mother's family lived at Number Ten Roberts Street, down the hill from where I live now and from where I am writing this story. It was an old two-story house that had a grocery store on the first floor and had rooms in the back and upstairs. After the older children had married or left home (and when money was tight), my great-grandmother would sometimes let out one of the upstairs rooms.

My grandmother watched the historic 1916 flood from the upstairs of Number Ten (as it was always called in the family), and the house looms large in the family mythology. There was a ghost who lived on the landing, if a sleeping ghost can be said to live. When the streetlights came on, he would appear on the old couch there, on his side with his back to the stairs.

No one in the family knew who he had been, but he wasn't a relative. He was the sleeping man, and they were comfortable with him being there. The house was torn down in the 1950s, and he must have faded with the dust of the old structure.

Here's his story, as I've imagined it.

His feet hurt, but then, his feet always hurt. The train from Opelika had been late, as usual, and he was going to be very late for his meeting with Mr. Green. That couldn't be helped because he was not in charge of the railroad's timetables, but he knew he would catch hell if he lost this contract.

He had been selling on the road his whole life. It seemed like a better life than the sharecropping his family had done, but now he was not so sure. He had a permanent sour stomach from the terrible food he ate, which was all he could afford when he was traveling. And he was always traveling.

There was a sharp pain in his shoulder as the train pulled into the depot. He raised his shoulders up toward his ears, hoping it would help. It did ease the pain a little, but he was still so very tired.

He pulled his suitcase and his sample bag from the shelf above his head and the shoulder pain came back, cold and quick. It faded as he adjusted his hat and turned to exit the carriage. There was a place he had stayed a few months back. Not far from the depot and the price was right. So he left the train and walked north, trying to remember the last time his feet didn't hurt. He had to walk almost a mile and the evening was hot and humid. He got slower and slower and was relieved to get to the point on Roberts Street where everything was downhill. It was dark by now and the streetlights were coming on. He was glad of the light—it lifted his heart. He wondered for a moment how angry Mr. Green would be and then decided that was a waste of his time. He'd be mad or he wouldn't, and there was nothing to be done about it.

The lady of the house was putting supper on the table, and she smiled to see her occasional lodger. She invited him to leave his cases in the hall and sit down with the family. He did so with a murmur about her kindness. He was one more mouth to feed in a formerly large family, and she was glad of the company too. He found he didn't have much of an appetite and blamed it on the sandwich he'd bought on the train. His stomach didn't feel right, and that pain in his shoulder had come back with a vengeance. He was glad of the strong coffee though, and even ate a little bit of pie when it was offered.

Finally he excused himself from the table and told the lady of the house that he would settle with her in the morning, if that was acceptable. It was, she said, a smile softening her broad face. She liked the nice man from Opelika, and he always had some good stories after he finished with his clients for the day. She told the youngest boy to take his cases up to the spare room, but he insisted on carrying the sample case himself. There were glass bottles of Mrs. Pymm's Patented Formula in there and he'd be in big trouble if they were broken.

The boy was up and down the stairs in a flash, but the salesman from Opelika took his time. He finally arrived at the simple room and saw that the bed was turned down and very inviting. He carefully set down the case and was about to sit down and take off his shoes, when he had a pain in his belly. This was not good. He looked for the pot under the bed and was glad to see it there. With a heavy sigh, he determined to go down to the kitchen and see if there was a glass of water with a little bicarb to ease his belly.

His aching feet were the least of his worries as he stumbled down the narrow hallway toward the stairs. Everything hurt all of a sudden and he grabbed the handrail hard, forcing himself to put one foot in front of the other. He made it down the first few stairs, but when he got to the landing and its lumpy old sofa, he suddenly stopped. He would sit here for a minute and see if he felt any better. He plopped down and looked at both sets of stairs. If he made it down to the kitchen, he might feel better. But then he would have to walk up all those steps back to his room. If he went back up the short section of the staircase, he could lie down on that bed and put his feet up. He knew he'd feel better in the morning, after a good night's sleep.

It was a puzzle.

It seemed his head was feeling heavier and heavier, and he finally gave in and stretched out on the sofa, drawing his knees up so he'd fit. He had his back to the rest of the world and the light coming in from the streetlight outside seemed exactly right. His feet weren't hurting now and his head felt light. The pain in his shoulder spread across his back and down into his chest and he closed his eyes. A little sleep now and then he'd get down those stairs for a nice bicarb. The pain started to fade and the light was so beautiful as he opened his eyes. He felt happy and pain free for the first time in recent memory. Then the salesman from Opelika closed his eyes again and stayed facing that beautiful light forever.

A Haint Tale: The Ticket Lady and Her Father

The old movie palaces of a bygone era are rare in our times. A very few have been transformed or incorporated into arts centers but most have met their wrecking ball fates through downtown development. This one—with the ghostly ticket lady—is now a parking lot for a bank. It was in the middle of a city block, all of which met its fate in the late 1970s.

The ticket area was a small enclosed cubicle in front of the entrance to the lobby. The ticket lady was there for years, from the time she was a young woman until she was past her prime. I remember she was very well put together, with piled-up hair and long gold fingernails. She was often smoking a cigarette, the blue smoke curling up from the ashtray and clouding the ticket booth.

Down the street from the missing theater is a cafeteria so legendary and beautiful that it has so far defied the developers. It was built in 1928 in classic Art Deco style, designed by a famous architect. When I was leading the ghost tour, I told the story of how haunted the place was. On one of the tours, someone got a picture of a faded African-American man in a waiter's jacket, walking with trays down the central staircase.

What do these two sightings have in common?

Between the theater that was and the cafeteria that still is, there is a splendid building with a frieze of strange faces above its long windows. The faces were modeled after people who paused to watch the craftsman as he worked on the building. It was built in 1895 and now is the home of a lawyers' office. It has a turret on the corner facing the street and it is an outstanding building.

Now we have our setting and our two characters. Let us explore their connection. The ticket lady was a sophisticated woman, independent, stylish. She continued to be a handsome woman as she aged, a fixture in the downtown scene. He was a man of his time who worked with dignity at a necessary job. A Black man in a small Southern town during the Jim Crow era.

What almost no one knew was that he was her father. In a time when passing for white was an emotionally complicated way of moving up in society, she had chosen to do so. And she worked only a block from his place of work so they could see each other, almost every day.

They would meet as if by accident at the turreted corner of that old building. He would have his head bowed, appropriately respectful, as she spoke to him. After a few moments they would go their own way, back to their separate lives.

He died first and the cafeteria was sad to lose a good worker. For months afterward she continued to walk down to the corner at the usual time, only to remember he wouldn't be coming, ever again.

She still makes that walk, on evenings when the moon is full, down to the corner of the turreted building. She waits there for a moment, but he never comes. She fades, only to return the following night, wishing to see the father she couldn't acknowledge.

A Haint Tale: The Running Children

The building I work in is an old hospital, and our little chapel is in the space that served as the hospital's morgue. I like to watch people's expressions as I tell them that. Then I remind them that people don't die in morgues—they died throughout the hospital, all of which is more likely to be haunted than the morgue. They seem relieved by that, until I tell them about the Running Children, the spirits right outside our door and also over by the only bathrooms on the lower level.

We first encountered them years ago while in a meeting. We could hear the sound of small feet pounding their way down the hall in front of our door. We heard muffled voices and giggling. We didn't think anything about it. We were in the building on a weekend and someone in an office down the hall must have brought their little ones in while the parent caught up on some work.

And then one of us saw them. Going quickly toward the bathroom, one of our volunteers had her head down as she walked. She heard a sound in front of her and looked up to see two children running ahead of her, their arms waving as they ran. The children were fading as she watched and soon disappeared. That's when we realized they were dead.

They don't seem scared at all. They seem to be running for the sheer pleasure of running, as children do. One is taller than the other, and we guess they must be three and five, or ages thereabouts.

Since they are often heard right outside our door, I have a theory about the Running Children. I think they were the children of someone who worked in the building, maybe a cleaner or janitor. The rooms that housed the laundry are across the hall from us—maybe their mother worked there. While their parent was working, they wandered a bit because they were in the basement, the least-used part of the hospital. Perhaps they hung around the morgue, scaring each other about the dead people on the other side of the door. Perhaps they waited until the person working in the morgue went out for a smoke break or for lunch. They saw their chance to sneak in. Then they saw a dead person, maybe more than one, and it scared the bejeezus out of them. They ran helter-skelter out of the room and down the hall as fast as their legs would carry them.

And they've kept doing it for all the years between then and now, imprinted forever in the halls of the lower level, the one with the morgue and the laundry.

Maybe that's the story of our Running Children. We don't know their story. We only know they are there sometimes, giggling, whispering, and running away.

A Haint Tale: Old Man Johnston's Angel Crown

You may have heard of an "angel crown," a little ring of feathers that is said to be found in the feather pillow of someone who has died and is heaven-bound. They are strange artifacts, to be sure, and ephemeral too. Many families have stories of an elder whose pillow contained such a blessed talisman but few were kept. There are a couple of good examples in the folk life collection at the Museum of Appalachia in Clinton, Tennessee. Being a thing of feathers, its likelihood of long-term survival was understandably slim.

Or maybe they weren't safe to keep around, these portals to the afterlife. Who knows what might make its way through that talisman and into the world of the living?

Old Man Johnston was well-known in his mountain community but he was not well loved. There had always been something peculiar about him, and his attitude was often harsh and uncompromising. He lived by himself in a two-story house that his father had built. It was high on a hill and had a turret-tower on the side of the house nearest the woods. It hadn't been painted in years and the front steps that used to creak were now bowed and broken. Mr. Johnston always used the back door, near the kitchen, to go in and out for his weekly trip to the Piggly Wiggly, which was about the only place he ever went.

He was estranged from his two children, who lived in cities in the North, far away. His wife had been dead for dozens of years, and he was lonely but stubborn. Those adult children sent him cards and even letters but he never responded, if he even opened them. Later they were found in boxes in his tidy bedroom, neatly put away in chronological order.

There came a cool autumn day when Mr. Johnston did not go to the Piggly Wiggly. No one really missed him that week because he was such a regular fixture that the staff, if they gave him a thought, would have concluded he'd gone through another checkout line. The week after, one of the older clerks did mention that she hadn't seen him that week, but they dismissed her worry, once more assuming someone else had checked out his pitiful groceries. After three weeks, the store manager remarked on it and decided he'd call his brother-in-law at the hospital and see if Mr. Johnston was sick. The brother-in-law was too busy to check right at that moment and then forgot all about it, as did the manager at the Piggly Wiggly.

So it was that a whole month went by before the mailman noticed a bad smell coming from the house and peered through the window on the front door to see the mail all piled up on the floor below the mail slot. The smell was stronger, and he backed away and went directly to the police department to make a report.

Mr. Johnston was dead in his iron bed, where he'd been for several weeks. The body was taken away and all the windows opened up to try to get some of the smell out of the place. The body was examined at the hospital and the cause of death was heart attack, though the people in the little town wondered that he'd had a heart at all. His children were contacted and they came home to bury their father and show some respect though they couldn't show love.

They decided they'd best go through the house and see what could be salvaged, now that most of the smell was gone. They found all sorts of strange and mummified creatures, some they couldn't even identify. There were jars of formaldehyde containing creatures from faraway lands. The brother and sister worked their way through all the odds and ends of their father's sad life and filled garbage bags with the things that couldn't be recycled and boxes with things to be donated to charity. They saved their father's bedroom for last and started it on a bright winter morning, fortified by strong coffee and big sausage biscuits from the diner. They promised themselves a good supper when this room was done, and they had a big box of heavy-duty garbage bags. The sister opened the big window even wider than before because they planned to toss the bags out the window and into the high grass of the side yard.

They started with the closet and were careful to go through the pockets of each old suit. The better ones went into a white bag for donations and the frayed and elder ones went into the black bags. Back and forth they went to the window, looking at the iron bed as they passed it by. All the bedclothes had been trashed when the body was removed, but one pillow had escaped the pile and was hidden halfway under the bed.

Next was the chest of-drawers and most of that was old under-pants, holey socks, and frayed T-shirts. These went into a black bag and out the window. They found a little stash of money rolled up in his pajama drawer. Not too much, a couple hundred dollars. They wondered what their father had done without in order to save that little dab of money.

At last there was nothing left to go through except the table by the bed. The brother picked up the edge of the pillow, tossed it on the old stained mattress, and slid the bedside table nearer the weak winter light from the window. That's when they found the boxes of cards and letters they sent for so many years, opened, read, filed away. They both felt unaccountably guilty, wondering if they could have, if they should have done more. The sister sighed at last and reached for the pillow that had cradled her father's head. She cried a little then and so did her brother. When she stood up the old pillow caught on the edge of the box spring and ripped. Goose feathers floated in the light breeze from the window but something stouter fell right to the floor.

The brother picked it up and held it out to his sister. It was a circle of feathers, mashed together to form a ring as wide as a man's hand. "It's an angel crown," she whispered. "It means he went to heaven." She was somehow happy about that. She reached her hand out and touched the little ring of feathers.

There was a jolt like electricity that shot through her arm and through the arm of her brother too. It was as if they had been struck by lightning, glued to the spot. That's when the sound began. Softly at first, a shrill but soft sound like the moan of a sick child. The siblings looked at each other, their eyes wide, unable to separate their hands or to drop the ring of feathers. The sound grew louder. Louder and louder. The shrieking filled the room, then filled the house, and the sister and brother felt as though they were falling into the feather crown, into an unknown and terrible place. They looked into each other's faces and saw each begin to fade, to flow into the ring. With a mighty effort they pulled away from each other and dropped the angel crown onto the floor. The shrieking stopped immediately. The siblings ran out of the room and down the stairs. They called a local charity and gave them the two hundred dollars in payment for throwing away the black bags and taking the others. They left the town where they were born and where they were almost lost, and they never returned again. Later in the winter, some homeless teenagers were squatting in the house and left some candles burning as they ran from the oppression of the place. It burned to the ground that night and the whole town was relieved.

Sometimes those angel crowns don't have a thing to do with angels or with heaven, and we need to keep that in mind about all sorts of oddments we may encounter in the houses of the dead.

A Haint Tale: The Brown Mountain Lights

The Brown Mountain Lights are an unexplained natural phenomenon that has lent itself to legend for a very long time. The Native people of the region—the Catawba—told stories about these strange orbs that are seen to float above and into Linville Gorge, as did Civil War–era reports. I've seen them myself on several occasions and wrote a play about them years ago. Here is a different interpretation of the Lights:

When you have finished your forestberry pie at Famous Louise's Restaurant, you can make your way up the road across 221, the narrow road that takes you to Wiseman's View. It's signposted, so don't worry about getting lost. I'll meet you at the second overlook.

The rocks in the low stone wall are smooth river rocks. The last of the late autumn sun warmed the ledge and I sit there, waiting for you. I have sat here so many times, waiting and watching. Before this vantage point was built, I sat on the flat rock south of here, the one that looks down into the gorge. Knowing you will linger over your coffee and will be late to our meeting, I rise from the ledge and follow the road downhill to the stand of pines. I smell it before I see it and smile as I step onto the soft and old bed of needles. I slept here so many years before, resting my head on the scented floor. The flat rock lies beyond and beckons me to its very edge, inviting me to peer down into the darkening ravine. The temptation to step into the cool air, float, and fall is compelling.

I laugh and step back then. Your car is on the road at last, and my feet find their way back to my original perch. Darkness has dropped onto the land. I hear wheels pull into the parking area and a car door opens and shuts. You are trying to make your way down the unfamiliar path in the dark, to show me you can. I like that about you. A soft gasp and then you turn on the flashlight feature on your phone, and I see you in the backlight. You've put on some weight since we first met and it suits you. You look sturdy now. Strong.

I take your hand at the top of the steps and you turn off the light without a word. Your eyes will soon adjust. I gesture in the direction of Table Rock and you turn to look. The silence between us is beautiful, both of us almost breathless in anticipation of the experience.

The night is perfect. Cool but not cold. A touch of mist in the air—not too much. If it were day, we'd see the smoke that rises out of the coves and lingers in the treetops. I remind you that this isn't a certain thing—sometimes folks wait and wait and it never happens. But I'm feeling lucky tonight, feeling the wavy energy that signals a strong showing, a transformation.

I sit down and pat the ledge, inviting you to rest your feet. You shake your head. You say you feel like you can see farther if you're standing, like a sailor in the crow's nest of an old-timey ship.

It is so quiet I fancy I can hear the river below. It was a surprisingly rainy late summer, and the river is whitewater here, more so than usual. The last of the cloud cover moves offstage and the sky is clear but moonless. Perfect.

I snap my fingers as I see the first glimmer over on Hawks Nest. I point and you turn to face the mountain, bending slightly at the waist.

"Do you see?"

You shake your head.

"Wait."

Another bright spot and another. They rise up for a moment and then sink slowly into the gorge, soon out of sight. So far away they could be mistaken for distant car headlights heading down the logging road.

You kneel on the ledge then and the dim silhouette of your head nods. You've seen them.

They continue to rise and tumble and we begin to perceive the delicate colors—blue, greenish, rose. They are languid as they move, and I feel an excitement in my guts, for this always means transformation is possible, indeed likely.

I hear your gasp as the first shy light rises directly in front of our stony perch. Tiny. Larger than a lightning bug but not by much. It floats up and dissipates six feet above our heads.

Another good sign.

The lightballs falling from Table Rock are larger now, easily seen. The colors remain pastel but more easily discerned. Green is most prevalent, second is blue. The rose-colored ones are rare and fine.

Another bright spot rises before us, larger than the first. It is green, an indistinct ball that holds a star in its heart, like a star sapphire does. It pauses there, hovering, so close it could be touched. You reach out your hand and it comes to rest on your flattened palm. Your face is reflected in the greenish glow and it immediately rises away. Away and gone.

You are smitten now and I turn from the lights to watch your enchantment. This is the first phase, the door opening on the possible.

More lights rise now, in a strangely orderly fashion, and you bend to grasp the ledge and stand up on it. Both hands stretch out now and the balls of light, night-moths, on your hands. The glow from their inner fire brightens your hands, then your arms and face, resting briefly and continuing to rise.

I marvel at the number of them. In all my years I have never seen such an offering, such a ritual. They gather round you as they rise from the river, soon covering you completely. I hear you laugh now, a pure silvery sound that is part bell, part birdsong.

Soon I see nothing but the green and blue of the lights and you seem to shrink, as the ones before you have done. A surprisingly swift one flies straight from Table Rock, winds its way across the space between and comes to rest in your center, forming a sweetly glowing star.

The joy in the air is palpable and your laugh comes to my ears a final time. You rise then, with all the rest—and disappear above my head, too far away to reach.

Such a night! Transformation! Salvation! Revelation!

I put one foot on the ledge and rise to stand where you stood. I reach my hands out in front of me and the lights come and cover me. In the echo of your final laugh, a rose light enters me. I am complete again, perfectly light, perfectly happy.

I rise and follow.

Conclusion

A few years ago, I spoke at a large conference in San Jose. Between sessions I sat in the hotel's café, drinking coffee and reviewing the schedule. A breathless young woman appeared at my elbow. Excuse me. Are you the Appalachian woman?

I nodded and smiled. I am an Appalachian woman. Want to sit down? She sat on the edge of her little chair and quickly told me about the place where she spent her childhood summers: her grandparents' hill farm in West Virginia. I wish I could sing you the song of her sweet and deep memories. Whip-poor-wills and jar flies and tree frogs. Spring water and hound dogs and big snakes. She called up long-cooking soup beans and biscuits so hot she couldn't eat them without burning the roof of her mouth. A big family Bible that got read every day and a garden full of the best tomatoes she ever ate. Warm from the sun, with too much salt.

Even the outhouse (surrounded by flowers!) and the never-ending chores (I helped gather the eggs every morning!) had a mystique, a glamour about them.

She leaned across the table after a while and whispered, Did you ever clog dance? I smiled. You did, didn't you? I stood up then and reached out my hand. My feet found the rhythm and she joined in, dancing on carpet to the music of a busy restaurant on a February morning in California, a continent away from our collective roots.

We are everywhere, as I am discovering. North, Midwest, South, West. And if we have left the hill country, we often carry memories—sometimes our own, sometimes our parents'—memories of life in a land softened by distance and made mythic by that distance, whether of time or space.

These mountains are old and new, which is where we began in this journey. I hope this book has gone a ways to help the reader understand and appreciate the ways that we've practiced for many generations, ways with food, music, homesteading, and magic.

There is much more to know, of course. We merely brushed the surface of so many things, and I hope your natural curiosity will lead you down the rabbit holes that hold most interest for you. If you have roots in this strange old land, trace them to where they originate. And if you are a newcomer here, please learn what you can about the place before you work too hard to change it. Because we don't change easily or quickly here, in spite of our best efforts.

You have stood as witness to what I called in the beginning the darkest and truest part of me—a part that is never healed and never entirely broken. Here in this much-maligned region, my ragged voyage and the wayfinding signs are clearer for the reading. And I hope you have learned of the land and the diverse folks who dwell here, in body or in spirit.

Recommended Resources

Books

Adams, Sheila Kay. *Come Go Home with Me.* Chapel Hill: University of North Carolina Press, 1995.

Blethen, H. Tyler, and Curtis W. Wood. *From Ulster to Carolina: The Migration of the Scotch-Irish to Southwestern North Carolina.* Raleigh: North Carolina Office of Archives and History, 1998.

Carmichael, Alexander, ed. *Carmina Gadelica: Hymns and Incantations.* Edinburgh: Floris Books, 1994.

Child, Francis James, ed. *The English and Scottish Popular Ballads.* 5 vols. Boston: Houghton Mifflin, 1882–98.

English, Ashley. *Canning and Preserving with Ashley English.* Homemade Living. Asheville, NC: Lark Books, 2010.

Erbsen, Wayne. *Log Cabin Pioneers.* Asheville, NC: Native Ground Music, 2001.

Green, Percy B. *A History of Nursery Rhymes.* London: Greening Co., 1899. https://books.google.com/books/about/A_History_of_Nursery_Rhymes.html?id=-USFcfPEBe4C.

Hone, William. *The Year Book of Daily Recreation and Information: Concerning Remarkable Men and Manners, Times and Seasons, Solemnities and Merry-Makings*. London: Ward, Lock, Bowden, 1892.

Kahn, Kathy. *Hillbilly Women*. New York: Avon, 1973.

Kephart, Horace. *Our Southern Highlanders*. Knoxville: University of Tennessee Press, 1976.

Ritchie, Fiona, and Doug Orr. *Wayfaring Strangers: The Musical Voyage from Scotland and Ulster to Appalachia*. Chapel Hill: University of North Carolina Press, 2014.

Sharp, Cecil. *English Folk Songs of the Southern Appalachians*. 2 vols. Windsor, CT: Loomis House Press, 2012.

Swell, Barbara. *Children at the Hearth*. Asheville, NC: Native Ground Music, 2008.

Ulrich, Laurel Thatcher. *A Midwife's Tale: The Life of Martha Ballard, Based on Her Diary, 1785–1812*. New York: Vintage Books, 1991.

Wigginton, Eliot, ed. *Foxfire*. 12 vols. New York: Anchor Books, 1972–2004.

Organizations, Heritage Centers, and Museums

American Society of Dowsers
184 Brainerd St.
PO Box 24
Danville, VT 05828
www.dowsers.org

Anne Hathaway's Cottage
The Shakespeare Centre
Henley St.

Stratford-upon-Avon
Warwickshire
CV37 6QW
www.shakespeare.org.uk

Appalshop
91 Madison Ave.
Whitesburg, KY 41858
www.appalshop.org

Foxfire Museum & Heritage Center
98 Foxfire Ln.
Mountain City, GA 30562
www.foxfire.org

John C. Campbell Folk School
1 Folk School Rd.
Brasstown, NC 28902
www.folkschool.org

Museum of Appalachia
2819 Andersonville Hwy.
Clinton, TN 37716
www.museumofappalachia.org

Museum of the Cherokee Indian
PO Box 1599
Cherokee, NC 28719
www.cherokeemuseum.org

Rural Heritage Museum
Mars Hill University
100 Athletic St.

Mars Hill, NC 28754
www.mhu.edu/museum

Podcasts

Wyrd Mountain Gals Podcast
www.wyrdmountaingals.podbean.com

Bibliography

Adams, Sheila Kay. *Come Go Home with Me*. Chapel Hill: University of North Carolina Press, 1995.

Bible. King James Version. King James Bible Online, 2007. https://www.kingjamesbibleonline.crg/.

Blethen, H. Tyler, and Curtis W. Wood. *From Ulster to Carolina: The Migration of the Scotch-Irish to Southwestern North Carolina*. Raleigh: North Carolina Office of Archives and History, 1998.

Carmichael, Alexander, ed. *Carmina Gaelica: Hymns and Incantations*. Edinburgh: Floris Books, 1994.

Child, Francis James, ed. *The English and Scottish Popular Ballads*. Boston and New York: Houghton, Mifflin and Company, 1882–98.

English, Ashley. *Canning and Preserving*. Asheville, NC: Lark Books, 2010.

Erbsen, Wayne. *Log Cabin Pioneers*. Asheville, NC: Native Ground Music, 2001.

Granik, Debra, dir. *Winter's Bone*. Los Angeles: Roadside Attractions, 2010.

Green, Percy B. "An Essex Charm for a Churn." In *A History of Nursery Rhymes*, 134. London: Greening Co., 1899. https://books .google.com/books/about/A_History_of_Nursery_Rhymes .html?id=-USFcfPEBe4C.

Hone, William. *The Year Book of Daily Recreation and Information: Concerning Remarkable Men and Manners, Times and Seasons, Solemnities and Merry-Makings*. London: Ward, Lock, Bowden, 1892.

Kahn, Kathy. *Hillbilly Women*. New York: Avon, 1973.

Kephart, Horace. *Our Southern Highlanders*. Knoxville: University of Tennessee Press, 1976.

———. "The Smoky Mountain National Park." *The High School Journal* 8, no. 6/7 (1925): 59–65, 69.

Jones, Lewis E. "There Is Power in the Blood." 1899. https:// hymnary.org/text/would_you_be_free_from_the_burden _jones.

Paris, Mike. "The Dixons of South Carolina." *Old Time Music* 10 (Fall 1973): 13–17.

Ritchie, Fiona, and Doug Orr. *Wayfaring Strangers: The Musical Voyage from Scotland and Ulster to Appalachia*. Chapel Hill: University of North Carolina Press, 2014.

Sharp, Cecil. *English Folk Songs of the Southern Appalachians*. 2 vols. Windsor, CT: Loomis House Press, 2012.

Smithers, Gregory. *Native Southerners: Indigenous History from Origins to Removal*. Norman, OK: University of Oklahoma Press, 2019.

Swell, Barbara. *Children at the Hearth*. Asheville, NC: Native
Ground Music, 2008.

Ulrich, Laurel Thatcher. *A Midwife's Tale: The Life of Martha Ballard,
Based on Her Diary, 1785–1812*. New York: Vintage Books, 1991.

Wigginton, Eliot, ed. *Foxfire*. 12 vols. New York: Anchor Books,
1972–2004.